When the Roof Caves In

LIVING TESTIMONIES SERIES

AN OMF BOOK

Copyright © OVERSEAS MISSIONARY FELLOWSHIP
(formerly China Inland Mission)
Published by
Overseas Missionary Fellowship (IHQ) Ltd.,
2 Cluny Road, Singapore 1025,
Republic of Singapore

First published 1985
Reprinted 1986, 1988

OMF Books are distributed by
OMF, 404 South Church Street,
   Robesonia, Pa. 19551, USA;
OMF, Belmont, The Vine,
   Sevenoaks, Kent, TN13 3TZ, UK;
OMF, P.O. BOX 177, Kew East,
   Victoria 3102, Australia;
and other OMF offices.

ISBN 9971-972-31-X

Printed in Singapore

cm 3K 2.88

Contents

DENIS LANE *has been a missionary in Malaysia and Singapore for 25 years. He is now OMF's Director for Home Ministries.*

When the Roof Caves in

I will never forget the time when, as a child of six or seven, I was having breakfast one day when the ceiling became mixed with the cornflakes. The sense of shock as lumps of plaster showered around us mingled with the feelings of fear about those other chunks that hung by a thread over our heads. My appetite disappeared with my security, and it all seemed like the end of the world. That was only a ceiling, and I was only a child. For many who read this book, the whole roof of life has cascaded down in a heap of rubble. You may be wondering what has hit you, and whether life can ever be the same again. We trust that the Lord will use this book to help you, and to enable you to realize that you are not alone in your agony.

People tend to put missionaries on pedestals and to feel that they do not face the same problems as ordinary folk, or even if they do they are such spiritual giants that they have no difficulty in coping. Paul demolished that idea in Acts 14:14,15.

The people of the city had just decided that he must be some sort of a god, and were about to worship him and his companion, Barnabas. The two men tore their clothes and rushed into the crowd, shouting, "Men, why are you doing this? We too are only men, human like you."

So you will read in this book of bereavement, cot death, accident, fire, sickness and separation. These and other roofs have caved in on missionaries in the course of their serving God. Some of these people are still working through the issues involved, for some roofs fall heavier than others. Others have come through the darkness into the light again. They want to encourage you to look to the "God and Father of our Lord Jesus Christ, the Father of compassion and the God of all comfort, who comforts us all in our troubles, so that we can comfort those in any trouble with the comfort we ourselves have received from God" (2 Cor. 1:3-4). Comforts, like problems, are meant to be shared.

In this opening chapter, however, I would like to examine with you some of the feelings that come to us all in times of distress and crisis, and to point the way to beginning to be able to cope with them. My theme comes from one of the most moving passages on suffering in the Bible: Psalm 22. In this psalm David expressed his own feelings, and the Spirit of God raised the outpourings of his heart to a new sublime level, by fitting those utterances to the experience of Jesus Christ upon the cross. No suffering has ever exceeded His. No suffering was less deserved. The one perfect human being who had done nothing but good found Himself rejected, cast out, beaten, spat upon, and nailed to die on the most infamous piece of wood in history. The psalm fits His case exactly, and in a measure I think you will find it also fits yours.

Let us then look at the feelings that afflict a person when the roof caves in.

The first feeling is a question: Why?

I take great comfort from the fact that Jesus Himself asked the very question in the opening words of this psalm when He hung upon the cross. He too asked "why?" "My God, My God, why have You forsaken Me?" You may feel guilty that you should even ask such a question. Surely, someone who can say "My God" in a personal sense, should not query His ruling of the universe? Surely such a person should be able to stand serene, as the tiles pour down around him. Yet Jesus asked that question, and in His case with the greatest justification. There was no reason for Him to die. He had harmed no one. He had never sinned against God. There was no earthly reason why His perfect body should be wracked with pain and tortured by thirst.

Asking the question is perfectly natural. We all ask it. There is nothing wrong, and everything human in doing so. We do not have to *stay* in verse one of this psalm, but that is usually the place where we begin. Fay Goddard tells us of the "cries and questions of my heart" when suddenly faced with the awful realization that she would never walk unaided again. God does not always answer our "why" questions, but He does understand our asking them. Jesus was given no answering voice as He hung upon the cross. The triumph and achievement hidden there could only be grasped by the hand of faith. The resurrection was still three days in the future.

From the sufferings of Job to the famines of Ethiopia, we still ask "why?" No easy answers are available. If we had them hidden away somewhere, someone in the history of the human race would have found them. But we can take comfort in the fact that it is the very reality of God and His love and grace that raises the question at all. I can answer the "why" question if there is no God. The reply is simple. If God does not exist, you and I are simply cogs in a vast predetermined machine, helpless pebbles on the beach, bound to be ground to sand under the merciless waves of time. Life has no meaning. We are just pieces left over from the first big impersonal bang, shrapnel from the explosion of creation. God's being and love *raises* the question.

A second common feeling is loneliness.

Do you know that feeling almost of resentment as you walk down the street and everyone else is going about their normal business, oblivious of the ache in your heart? Have you not felt that sense that it is almost blasphemous for people actually to be enjoying themselves, when your roof has caved in? You feel that you are all alone and no one can realize the depth of your hurt.

The first verse of Psalm 22 expresses this feeling too by the cry, "Why have you forsaken me?" Even God seems distant. The sufferer is all alone, abandoned to his or her fate. God has forgotten to be gracious. Later on, in verse 11, David said, "Do not be far from me, for trouble is near and there is no one to help." That sums up this feeling of loneliness. I have little doubt that there were other people around, many of them wanting to help, good well-intentioned individuals. But what David was conscious of was the nearness of the trouble and the inability of anyone really to be able to touch it. Often those very people who come to comfort you in your troubles are aware of their inability to help. They do not know what to say and fumble with cliches or stand around in embarrassed silence. In some situations like this you are all alone, and in your loneliness may pray with David and his greater son, "Why are you so far from saving me, so far from the words of my groaning?" Every mother who, like Lois Michell, has just said goodbye to her boys and had to make a long journey back to an "empty nest", has known what that loneliness is.

Some paths are only wide enough for one person at a time. The path of suffering is one of those. However much others try to help and want to help, the track has to be walked alone. For Jesus on the cross, this sense of loneliness and separation from the Father with whom He had walked and communed every minute of every day of His life, was part of the deepest agony. We never have to be quite that lonely, and we know He has walked this way before and walks it with us now.

A third common feeling is self-deprecation and guilt.

In looking for the answer to the "why" question we often turn the searchlight on ourselves and come to some unwarranted conclusions. In the psalm, David recounted the experience of his ancestors. "In you our fathers put their trust; they trusted and you delivered them. They cried to you and were saved; in you they trusted and were not disappointed." But of course they were different, he implied, going on to draw the false conclusion, "But I am a worm and not a man, scorned by men and despised by the people" (verses 4-6).

Perhaps you have made the same deduction. The good things happen to other people. Theirs are the prayers that get answered. They trusted and were delivered. But that has not happened to you. You prayed for healing and the person died. You prayed for deliverance, and none seemed to come. There can be only one conclusion, since it would be wrong and useless to accuse God. You must be someone who is different, a worm and not a full human being. Then you begin to think of all the ways in which you can see yourself as a worm, and even imagine that other people are seeing you that way too.

Jim and Doreen Tootill speak of the "if onlys" that went through their minds after their little girl was drowned in the boating accident. Nick Watkins tells us, "As if it wasn't enough to wrestle with grief, guilt also raised its ugly head... We would go over the events preceding Matthew's death, scrutinizing each detail, and inevitably Raili would come to the conclusion that she was to blame." The dynamics of grief are common to the human race, and blaming yourself is a common symptom. Jesus was treated like a worm, and for Him the cross was the ultimate identification with all that makes us wormlike, and the doorway to our deliverance. Yet still, even for those who trust in Him, the feelings of guilt and unworthiness come piling in during roof cave-ins.

A fourth feeling is hopelessness.

David felt despised by the people. Some even seized the opportunity to mock his faith. "He trusts in the Lord, let the Lord rescue him. Let him deliver him, since he delights in him" (verse 8). His feelings came out again later as he said, "I am poured out like water... my heart has turned to wax, it has melted away within me... You lay me in the dust of death" (verses 14,15). People seemed to have written him off. He wondered if he had the strength to face another day. You may have felt like that too. Pain and grief have emotional overtones that wear away at the spirit and undermine the strength. We have all had those times when our heart seems to have melted away like wax in the fire and our resistance has crumbled or dissolved into self pity. This feeling of hopelessness can attack us parti-cularly in those circumstances when one trouble seems to pile upon another. Lynn McNickle writes, "How desolate I felt — my three children all gone and my husband lying on his back in agony, unable to move without excruciating pain... Why do we go through these agonies...?"

Jesus on the cross could quote the words of Psalm 22 as an exact description of the mockery and suffering He endured. His strength was literally dried up, and His tongue would have stuck to the roof of His mouth in the dehydration of crucifixion. They did pierce His hands and His feet, and they did cast lots for His garments. He did not have the strength to face another day in the desperation of His human condition. He knows what you feel and more, when the roof caves in.

A fifth feeling is a sense of being on stage.

By this I mean that feeling we have when we think everyone is watching us, noting our reactions and perhaps commenting upon them. The psalm describes this sensation as being like standing in the bull ring, surrounded by huge, hostile beasts, or being encircled by lions eager for the prey. At the very least, it is like being in a crowd of snapping dogs. Not all of us feel as though the surrounding crowd is quite so hostile, but often we do feel as though we are in the spotlight, and in the middle of what we are enduring we would give anything to be just a normal member of the crowd. Gill Stedeford endured the agony of uncertainty whether her husband would live or die, and had to face it in the midst of a whole community. Fortunately they were a loving, caring community who provided help, but it is never easy to have to face your pressures in the light of everyone else's knowledge.

Jesus on the cross faced the very worst kind of publicity, openly stripped and exposed, hung up for all to see, while the guards underlined that He was finished by gambling away His clothes. He had to endure it right by the public highway with rough voices mocking His unwillingness to save Himself. He knows what you endure when your suffering is on centre-stage.

Not all of us endure all of these feelings, but I am thankful that David recorded them for us in this psalm, and that Jesus knows what it is to face them all and come through victorious. The point I would make is that these feelings are perfectly consonant with our human nature. We cannot stop their coming. Feelings are feelings and come unannounced, but if we know they are normal we can live with them and overcome them. Some may last for longer than others, depending on the trauma attached to our particular roof's caving in. Some, like the example with which I began, are more like ceilings falling down, dramatic at the time but soon recovered from. Others are longer-term hurts like bereavements, and others affect the whole of the future course of our lives. Is there then no help we can glean from this psalm to strengthen our resolve and minister to our needs?

I have already indicated, and we all already know, that there are no easy or complete answers, no magic wands to wave, no mother's kiss to dissolve the pain in an instant. We have instead to look long-term, and even from the perspective of eternity before we can find satisfying solutions. Paul, in the context of reasons for not losing heart, said this: "Our light and momentary troubles are achieving for us an eternal glory that far outweighs them all. So we fix our eyes not on what is seen but on what is unseen. For what is seen is temporary, but what is unseen is eternal" (2 Cor. 4:16-18).

If this life is all there is, then there are no answers. Time and time again the innocent suffer and the guilty seem to go free. Time and time again people endure a life of suffering, and some rise to magnificent heights in coping with their handicaps, but if our horizons are limited to this life we have little hope. David however points us to his own confidence, a confidence that burns to incandescence in the life, death and resurrection of the Lord.

He found his first hope in the history of God's people.

We find it very easy to think of our own situation as unique. One of the values of Christian fellowship lies in sharing our feelings with one another and discovering that, far from being alone in our experiences, we live in a world full of people who have experienced them too. We have already looked at verses three to five, which speak of the trust placed in God by previous generations, a trust that was not disappointed. The historical perspective helps us to see things in a new light.

Christians in China have just been through one of the most difficult periods of persecution in the history of the Christian Church, but many of them found comfort in books like the Revelation, written during a time of Roman oppression. At the time, many ex-missionaries thought that all their work had been wasted and the church had been destroyed, but now we can see a vastly multiplied and greatly strengthened church. Individual Christians lived and died without seeing the effect of their witness during those terrible days, but when we look over the whole scene with the hindsight of history we can see that their suffering was by no means in vain.

Therefore, when the roof caves in and we are tempted to look inwards at our feelings and our problems, we do well to look instead at the experience of the previous ages of God's people. To pit our limited, temporary experience against the verdict of history cuts us off from the comfort of knowing that in the end God is totally trustworthy, and what we cannot see now will be made plain later in time or in eternity. The Bible does not pretend that suffering can be avoided. Indeed it tells us that it is given to us "on behalf of Christ not only to believe on Him, but also to suffer for Him" (Phil. 1:29).

He found his second hope in his own personal history.

David put it like this: "...You brought me out of the womb; You made me trust in You even at my mother's breast. From birth I was cast upon You; from my mother's womb You have been my God" (verses 9,10). None of us would be alive at all if God had not sustained our life from the very beginning, when we were utterly helpless. One of the stories in this book is about that mysterious phenomenon we now call a cot death. That could have happened to any one of us in our own infancy. When you look back, I am sure there are instances in your own experience that cause you to acknowledge that but for the grace of God you would not be here. I had concussion three times as a child. Some of my friends may think that explains a lot, but each one of those occasions could have been fatal. A child from the same primary school in my home town was killed by a bomb one night, and I often thought that that could have been me.

Our own experience of the mercies of God should tell us that what we are facing at this moment is not the only side to life. We may not understand what is going on, but we must allow the evidence on the other side to have its true value. We cannot reject or doubt the truth about God and His love now, without contradicting both the whole of human history and our own personal one.

He found his final and main hope in the truth of resurrection.

The mood of the psalm changes after verse 21. Beginning with a resolve to testify to God's character in the congregation, and moving through an invitation to praise the Lord, it reaches in verse 24 a confident assertion that God "has not despised or disdained the suffering of the afflicted one; he has not hidden his face from him but has listened to his cry for help." This change of mood seems strange after the agonizing cry with which the psalm began. But the mood brightens still further, stating that "All the ends of the earth will remember and will turn to the Lord, and all the families of the nations will bow down before him, for dominion belongs to the Lord and he rules over the nations."

Only in the light of the resurrection of Jesus Christ can the latter half of the psalm be understood. The first part was literally fulfilled in astounding detail at the time of the crucifixion. It is perfectly natural therefore to see the second half in terms of His resurrection. Just before He ascended to heaven after forty days of revealing Himself to His disciples, He claimed that all authority on heaven and earth had been given to Him, and that fits exactly with the verses quoted above. Suffering and death were not the end. Evil did not have the last word. He who died in agony and shame rose in glory and majesty. The sting of death has been drawn, and the sting of death is sin, for which He died. Had He not risen again we would have no hope, but now in Him we have an everlasting hope.

I said earlier that if our horizons are limited to this life, then we are left with nothing but a large question mark over all the demolished roofs of human experience. This psalm, and the historical fact of the resurrection that it foreshadows, give us grounds for firm confidence, not only that this life is not all there is but also that suffering is not final and unanswerable. Jesus faced the worst kind of suffering in every way. He went through physical anguish, spiritual desertion, emotional alienation from others, all for something of which He was not guilty. We can sometimes bear up under suffering we have brought upon ourselves, but unjust suffering is hardest of all to bear. In Jesus' case, He not only did not deserve it but freely took it on Himself on behalf of you and me, who did deserve it for our constant rebellion against God. God honoured that sacrifice, took Him from the stranglehold of death and opened a door to hope and life, not only for Him but for all those who rest and trust in Him.

When therefore the roof caves in, and we find echoes of our own hearts' feelings in this psalm and in the experience of Jesus Christ upon the cross, we do well to look beyond the cross to the resurrection; beyond the suffering to the life. Eternity is not a vague optimism about life beyond death, but a solid reality, secured for us by the resurrection of Jesus Christ. Someone *has* gone beyond and come back. Someone *has* triumphed over death and suffering. Someone *has* been vindicated from the injustices that He received.

Our feelings will still come. You may well find the "why" question welling up in your heart. You may still feel that somehow you are different, a worm and no man. You may still feel that loneliness, or sense of being on the centre of the stage. Such feelings cannot be controlled, but they can be healed. Time plays its part in that, and so does the love and care of those around us.

You can also assist the process of healing if you set your mind and eye in the right direction. The testimony of God's people through the centuries has been that however dark the day, God brings His light into it in the end. The testimony of your own experience tells you that God has kept you many times before and is well able to keep you now. The testimony of the resurrection tells you that death and suffering are not final. There is an eternity and a new life beyond. The Author of that life is living still, despite the worst that sin and evil could do. He lives to come to you with the comfort of His Holy Spirit, and the healing of His love. The testimonies that follow will tell you how others have found that comfort to be so real. They had their feelings too, and sometimes the feelings come back, but the comfort is real and strong.

Dorothy Beavan, in the account of her accident, tells how time and time again the small verse came to her in different situations: "Be still and know that I am God." For some who read these words, this may be what you need. Perhaps you have been just too busy to listen to Him, take notice of Him, worship Him, seek for Him. For you Jesus Christ may be simply a figure of history and no more. Maybe you need to be still and to realize that the greatest sufferer this world has known not only suffered for you but lives today to draw near by His Holy Spirit and to bring you the healing of His love. Jesus lives! In Him and His death and resurrection we find our hope. You will not find it anywhere else. "Be still and know..."

Colleen Davis, *from Canada, has worked in Thailand and Singapore.*

A
Shot
Was Fired

There I was crying again. How many times was this now? Three? Four? Koos was away overnight again. That had never bothered me before. But somehow, since returning recently to the town of Thatako for our third term in Central Thailand, I had begun to lie awake at night thinking of what I would do if something happened to Koos. I was certain I couldn't carry on without him. Life wouldn't be worth living. I knew I would just fall apart. And so I cried.

This time, as each time before, the Lord brought to me the thought, "When someone dies you cry then. Not before it happens. Satan is trying to depress you." And so the crying stopped, relief flooded over me and I slept. But in the morning I was still left with the certainty that if Koos were ever killed I would fall apart.

Khao Din. A remote village, just a shop and a few homes. To get there Koos and his brother Bill rode their motorbikes easily the nineteen paved kilometers to Phai Sali. The next 22 kilometers to Khao Din varied in time from 45 minutes bouncing over the hard packed dirt ruts of the dry season, to two and a half hours sliding through the numerous floods and mud baths of the rainy season.

With our co-workers, David and Jenny Robinson, we had earlier decided not to visit Khao Din because of the lawlessness there. The police had no influence, and a group of town bullies appeared to control the area. It had the reputation that you could be killed there for the sake of a motorbike. No one travelled after dark, and dark comes early in the tropics.

However, during our furlough when Bill and Lois Fietje came to work with the Robinsons, a lady shop owner in Khao Din became a Christian. Her changed life so affected her customers that many wanted the missionaries to come to teach, staying overnight once each week as they knew was done in Phai Sali.

With the Robinsons now on furlough and our family just resettling, Bill made the first visit to Khao Din alone. About 35 people had gathered expectantly to wait for him. Although Bill returned next morning with a high temperature and the accompanying symptoms of dengue fever, his enthusiasm also ran high. So many wanted to believe. But believe what? They knew so little. After prayer, we felt led to take advantage of this rare openness.

And so the routine developed. Almost every Saturday afternoon, after praying with their families for protection, Bill and Koos would set off on motorbikes for Phai Sali where they usually picked up someone from Khao Din. They felt that this might reduce the chance of robbery. They rode on to Khao Din, made a few visits, showered and ate with the shop owner's family. After dark, when people had gathered, there was singing, teaching, sharing, questions and prayer. After the more formal time, groups would form to talk and ask more questions. When the others had left, Bill and Koos joined the circle of those staying overnight, sitting on the floor sipping hot tea (you have to boil the water anyway) and munching peanuts. Then welcome sleep would come as they stretched out on bamboo mats on the wooden floor. In the morning there would be Bible reading and prayer together, a quick rice breakfast, sometimes more visiting, then the return to Phai Sali or Thatako for the Sunday morning service.

As several grew in the Lord, so opposition also grew. Rocks were thrown on the roof during meetings. Once as some folk were returning home in the dark, gunshots were fired over their heads. We were conscious of danger on the roads. Before leaving Saturday afternoon, Koos had said at different times, "I'm leaving my watch and ring here in this drawer." Or, "If anything happens to me, here's the money for the electrician." And later, "I've paid the electrician. If anything happens, don't pay him any more."

And then what I had feared did happen. Koos had gone that Saturday on his own, as Bill and Lois were doing language study in Bangkok. After the meeting Koos had joined three or four others on the floor for tea and peanuts. As they were talking a shot was fired straight at Koos through the slatted wall of the verandah. Mercifully, he entered the Lord's presence instantly. There was no robbery, no theft. Someone had wanted the evangelist stopped.

It was two a.m. Sunday when I heard Mrs Roy calling at the front door. She was one of the first Christians from Phai Sali. Koos had often stayed in her home, and she in ours. As I pulled back the folding iron door I saw a pickup truck carrying about seven men, driven by the husband of the shop owner in Khao Din. No one travels alone after dark.

Mrs Roy had difficulty in bringing herself to break the news. As I tried to get an explanation of her presence at that hour, she repeatedly asked irrelevant questions. Was the bank clerk here? Had I seen the Christian teacher? Finally she forced herself to say, "He's been shot dead."

"Who?" I demanded, thinking, *If only Koos were here. He'd know what to do.*

After a prolonged silence during which I kept asking, "Who? Tell me who?" she finally whispered Koos's name.

Our natural reaction was to cling to one another and cry. But almost immediately the Lord reminded me of Ruth Wyss's experience in North Thailand. She and Thai friends had come upon the body of her husband Peter, who had also been shot. I had heard from others that the Lord had spoken to her about how important her reaction was in front of those tribal people. And now it was my reaction that was so important. Koos and I, like Peter and Ruth, had taught that the death of a Christian was not to be feared; the spirit of the departed one was gloriously with the Lord, not hovering nearby on earth.

Excusing myself from Mrs Roy's embrace, I sat on one of the chairs that Martina and Mark had helped arrange Saturday evening for the Sunday worship service. Briefly, I prayed for the Lord's comfort and peace. I asked Him to help me to know what to do next and to be calm enough to do it.

After this I was able to ask Mrs Roy calmly for the details of Koos's shooting. Then together we decided she should direct the truck to the Christian teacher's home. He came in his car, then as there were no telephones in Thatako went on to the police box where they called through to the police box in Paknampho, and from there Alan and Averil Bennett, OMF superintendent for Central Thailand, were alerted. The teacher then drove the eighty kilometers to the OMF hospital at Manorom — no telephones there either.

From then until late in the evening our home was a hive of activity. Local Christians soon arrived to be with me. About four a.m. Alan and Averil arrived with fellow missionary Rosemary Harding. At daybreak Alan left for Khao Din with some of the Christian men, soon followed by other missionary colleagues from Manorom. By eight a.m. Koos's brother Bill arrived from Bangkok with Ian Murray, then director for Thailand. After making sure I was all right and in good hands, they too followed on. By this time all Thatako knew what had happened to Koos, and it seemed that most of the town was milling around inside and outside the house. As well as caring for Mark, Martina and her own little Kristina, Averil organized our housegirl to prepare food. Rosemary spoke with the Christians who knew her as she had been coming weekly to teach Home Bible Seminary lessons. This left me free to speak with the many townspeople, both good friends and strangers, who came to talk.

By midmorning things had quieted somewhat and Rosemary led a short service for those who had come for the regular Sunday meeting, all ladies as the men had gone on to Khao Din. By now other missionaries and Thai Christians were arriving from farther away, and the house was still a hub of activity. Midafternoon Bill and I drove with Rosemary, whose advanced knowledge of Thai was a real aid to us, to the Phai Sali police headquarters to be questioned for the police report. That evening we had another service with Bill, Alan and Ian for all the Christians now present. Averil stayed with me overnight while the other OMFers returned to Paknampho and Bangkok. The Thai Christians returned home or stayed with friends in Thatako.

Throughout that whole eventful day the Lord kept me in perfect peace. His comfort and calm did not fail. And so it was over the next busy week, with a memorial service at Manorom followed by the funeral in Bangkok. I shall always be grateful for the loving support of Bill and Lois, to other OMFers who took over all the arranging of the services, and to Ian Murray and Arnold Melbourne for attending to innumerable administrative details.

Then there was a week-long trip to Chefoo, the school for missionaries' children in Malaysia, where our eldest child Michael was in grade four. He didn't want to leave Chefoo yet, so we returned to Bangkok without him in time to welcome my mother from Canada. Together over the next four or five weeks we packed up our house, sold many large household items, did Christmas shopping for Canada, exchanged many sad farewells and even arranged a four-day rest at OMF's beautiful holiday home right on the beach.

Two weeks before Koos's killing, a senior teacher in Thatako had also been shot. His family and friends were in a turmoil, his wife at times almost hysterical. The huge funeral, which Koos attended, offered no comfort to the mourners. The town angrily sympathized with the distraught family, calling for revenge.

And then the murder of a Christian. What a difference! There was grief at the sudden loss of a special person. But this time there was calm, the comfort that Koos was with the Lord, the promise that one day all we Christians would see him again and the assurance that the Lord would provide for his own. The whole town buzzed with the tremendous contrast.

Michael came up to Thailand mid-December with the other Chefoo children, and within a few days we were back in Canada, staying at first with my parents and then setting up our own home. As in Thailand, so here in Canada we were surrounded with love and care from relatives, friends, our church family and the OMF family. The Lord's peace and comfort was just as real to me as it had been in Thailand. Surprisingly, this created a problem. There was veiled and unveiled disbelief that I could be so calm. Surely I was just putting on a front? Inside, I must be in a turmoil, and I should give vent to my feelings or I was sure to break under the strain. Was I showing proper respect to Koos's memory? Didn't I miss him?

And so I started to question myself. Was I just deceiving myself? Should I be showing more grief? In the Lord's perfect timing I received a letter just then from a lady who had been widowed suddenly in her early twenties some years previously. She told of how the Lord had upheld her so wonderfully, so that she had said to her pastor, "I don't understand myself. I expected to go to pieces. It's not natural." To which he replied, "No, it's not natural. It's supernatural." Joyfully I thanked the Lord for His confirmation that my peace truly was from Him.

While I was still in Thailand, and even more so after returning to Canada, the Lord brought to me over and over the words "trust" and "wait". They shouted at me from sermons, letters and conversations. As I read all the familiar Bible passages about trusting the Lord and waiting for Him to bring something to pass, it seemed as if they were written just for me. I could picture myself as a little stick-figure in a cartoon with two thought balloons floating above my head reminding me — "trust, wait." I was expecting something, but I didn't know what.

During this time life was generally happy for us. Michael and Mark were enjoying the Christian school across the street. We were all involved in activities at our home church, Forward Baptist in Cambridge, which had generously offered to support us until Martina was school age and I could return to teaching. We spent time with family and friends. My parents were able to move next door to us, and Koos's parents were just a few blocks away. There were occasional speaking engagements, a weekly Bible study and even swimming lessons. I was enjoying life.

Then one evening I received a phone call from Rob Davis. It was as if the Lord hit me over the head with a hammer saying, "This is it! This is what you have been waiting for."

With his wife Margaret, Rob had served with OMF in Japan, in the Canadian office and for two and a half years as Director for Finance and Administration in Singapore. When Marg's illness was diagnosed as cancer their family returned to Toronto, where they were surrounded with practical love and concern by family, Melrose Baptist Church and friends until the Lord called Marg to Himself.

Rob and I were married in 1983, merging into one family with seven children who were then aged — Beth 12, Michael 11, Stephen 10, Jon Mark 8, Mark Koos 6, Martina 4, and Jamie 3. In January

1984 we travelled to Singapore where Rob again took up the reins as DFA.

The Lord's comfort has been and still is very real to me. That doesn't mean that I don't miss Koos, or that waves of revulsion at the horror of a real murder don't sometimes wash over me. But as my Heavenly Father has been faithful to me in the past, now I count on Him to be faithful in this new chapter of my life.

Fay Goddard *edits the OMF magazine* East Asia
Millions *in our USA office*

... *In any way He chooses*

Everything was perfect — almost, anyway. With sunshine firming up the ankle-deep mud that the rainy season had made of the jungle trails, I was settling into the spanking new house the Buhid Christians of the area had built to welcome me back to the Philippines. Already I sensed spiritual growth in the little church group, though they had been without missionary help most of the year I had been away for furlough. Behind me were five years of language learning and of getting to know the culture. Now, having freshly rededicated myself to the Lord for His "whatevers," I was looking forward almost with excitement to the term of missionary service ahead of me in the mountains of Mindoro Island.

I loved my house, standing tall on its stilts on the edge of a ridge overlooking a deep valley and a jungle-covered mountain range beyond. Lovingly custom-built for me, it had a grass roof with shaggy edges untrimmed, a ridge pole high enough to clear my blonde head, and a ladder stairway instead of the usual Buhid slanted pole. The house was small — I could just about reach each of the two side walls with my arms outstretched. But lengthwise, with the footlocker which was my one piece of furniture across one end, there was plenty of room for me to stretch out full length on the bamboo-slat floor to sleep. Three stones set into a mud slab on a shelf just outside my window provided a place to cook; a propped shutter overhead kept the fireplace dry. Best of all, my home was just off the trail that cut across the second-year field to the spring where the tiny community drew its water; that meant a steady stream of visitors.

Only two shadows dimmed the sunlight of those days. The first was a letter from the OMF superintendent informing me that I would have to work alone for the foreseeable future, as there simply was no one to fill the gap. My senior, Marie Barham, had died of cancer a year or so before I went on furlough. The second was that my Buhid friends were struggling with hunger and sickness in these weeks just before harvest. I wasn't happy about living alone and puzzled why God had not answered my prayer for a fellow worker. I was discovering, however, that with no one to talk to but tribal neighbors and visitors, my language ability was picking up quickly. And, despite their hunger, my neighbors in the little house a few yards downhill often stopped in with offerings of boiled green cooking bananas. I hated the bananas but ate them, aware of how precious food was just then. In turn I divided my bread supply with them; so the giving was that of mutual friends. My aloneness was working out for good.

But now, after only a week in my new house, I was tucking my few belongings into the footlocker, preparing for an unscheduled trip to the lowland base I shared with Bob and Joy Hanselman, who worked with another branch of the tribe further south. One of the Buhid had received a letter from a Tagalog lowlander and, being unable to read, brought the letter for me to decipher. "Read it again," he urged. As I did, I saw the glances passing from one Buhid to another among the listeners. When I read the message at their request a third time, exactly the same as the first and second time, they were impressed even more. Suddenly they were ready to learn to read, something they had firmly resisted for the eight years since Marie Barham had initially perspired her way into their mountains. But this turnabout had caught me by surprise; I was stuck without a firm alphabet to use in writing their language. I had to make the trip to find Joy, the linguist of the team, and check with her about factors like whether we would need six vowels or whether three would do. I hoped only that I could hitch a ride on a logging truck or find a weapon's carrier bus for the final eleven kilometers once I had made it to the base of the mountain on foot.

"I am going now," I called Buhid style to the family next door. As I headed into the morning sun, I never dreamed that I would never see them or my mountain house again.

Happily Bob and Joy with their two little ones turned up at our lowland base, relieving me of the need to make the wearisome trek to the Batangan River to find them. But we never did settle the alphabet question. I woke up the first Monday we were together feeling really rotten. "I'll rock John if you'll do the dishes," I bargained with Joy after breakfast. My handwashing soaked unfinished in the shower room. The baby's fussing gave me the excuse I was looking for to plunk my aching form into the old wooden rocking chair on the front porch. By afternoon I was flat on my cot, and when two-and-a-half-year-old James came in and climbed onto my stomach, I had soon had enough of his bouncing. Tuesday a pounding headache and a strange burning sensation on my lower spine sent me to the missionary medicine book for self-diagnosis. Did I have *polio*? The symptoms fit. By Wednesday I wondered as I struggled back from the outhouse if it would be the last time I would ever walk. That evening, alarmed when even the codeine they had gotten from a doctor in town failed to touch the throbbing pain in my head, back and knees, Bob and Joy made a frantic search for transportation to evacuate me to Calapan, the provincial capital.

About sunset Wednesday my companions loaded me, cot and all, into a battered and ailing minibus. A morphine shot made the bumpy ride north bearable, even a bit of an adventure. About 2:15 a.m. we arrived unannounced and without working headlights at OMF Mindoro superintendent's house in Calapan. By daybreak I could neither sit up nor turn over.

So it was really no surprise when that afternoon, after a flight to Manila, doctors confirmed that I did indeed have polio. The week before I had hiked from the mountains; now I was all but helpless. Life had come to a full stop. I was twenty-nine, unable even to hold a full glass of water.

The impact of what my illness would mean to my future didn't really hit me, however, until three months later when in Seattle the doctor came to help me order my very own personal wheelchair. All the hard work and therapy in the world would not erase the reality that I would be handicapped, severely so, for the rest of my life.

How was I to cope with such a staggering realization? What could keep the frustration of my inability to do what I wanted to from shoving me into self-pity? Sentimental platitudes would not now answer the cries and questions of my heart, any more than they did during my three months in the Manila Sanitarium.

One thing I was very thankful for from the start: only days before I spent that one week in the mountains among the Buhid, I had taken time to kneel down in my bedroom at our lowland base and reaffirm the Savior's lordship in my life, expressing my willingness for Him to use me in any way He chose. At that moment at my bedside I was happily conscious of being right square in the middle of God's will. Surely now I needn't worry that polio was a punishment for something. Somehow

I had to believe that God had simply taken me at my word and had a plan.

What sentiment couldn't do, God's Word did. His promises hadn't changed. The grace was still there for the taking. My personal relationship to the Lord was intact. All the working capital I had ever had that was worth anything was still available. With God's leading and grace I could surely manage the frustrations.

And I had a model: fellow missionary John Thompson had contracted polio in the Philippines four years before. Visitors to the Thompson home in Waynesboro, Pennsylvania, came away buoyed in spirit, even finding it hard to pity the man on the rocking bed who could not lift a single finger. I had visited John and Juanita during furlough, and I remembered.

Joy of high quality sweetened the whole nine months I spent in rehabilitation at the University of Washington Hospital. I was aware that God had just changed my mission field. Instead of g-stringed, barefoot Buhid, He had put me right in the middle of a group of people whose lives had been shattered by accidents, crippling disease, and foiled suicide attempts — teenage boys paralyzed from the neck down in falls on the ski slopes or in twisted auto wrecks, housewives felled by strokes and multiple sclerosis, young adults who had maimed themselves by leaps from heights or by drug overdose — and the physicians, therapists, and psychologists who were trying to patch their lives back together.

I have never had a happier nine months, frustrations and all.

Having walked out of the University Hospital triumphantly, though very fearfully, on crutches, I was unprepared for the depression that hid the sun a few weeks later, after I had arrived at OMF headquarters in Philadelphia. "Come," the mission leaders had written, "and we will find something for you to do," and my brother Pat and I had driven across country to Pennsylvania in my hand-control-equipped Oldsmobile. The "something ... to do" turned out to be stuffing envelopes, affixing stamps, and the like. In fact, office personnel were hard put to it to find enough to keep this non-trained office worker busy. I was a fifth wheel. Here I was at age thirty, a continent away from home and half a world away from where I wanted to be, and filling my days with inconsequential odd jobs. I was indeed on the shelf. Tears blurred the early fall scene out my bedroom window. "Why, Lord?" I cried.

Though my prayer that afternoon was more protest than petition, my heavenly Father gently reminded me of Job and of Satan's accusation. "When you were in the Philippines, you were serving Me, but you were also doing what you wanted to do most. As with Job, Satan isn't convinced of your motives in claiming me Lord," He explained. I saw the point. "Now I want you to show Satan that he is wrong. I want you to do for Me what you don't like doing, and I want you to do it with joy." I couldn't help remembering my vow never to work in an office.

"Okay, Lord," I submitted, "I'll do it." And I made up my mind to obey.

Within days I had my hands full with all the challenge that God and I could handle: I was given the job of producing the mission's magazine, *East Asia Millions*. But first, God had required my willingness to keep on stuffing envelopes for the rest of my life if that pleased Him. Now, more than twenty years later, I am still putting the magazine together — editing the material, doing the layout, and seeing that it is properly ready for printing. The joy is still there. God has developed gifts that were withering from disuse, some I didn't know I had, and has given me a full satisfying ministry — every bit as satisfying as preaching and discipling among the Buhid I loved and still love in the highlands of Mindoro, Philippines. To think I once feared giving Him the full reins of my life!

Graeme & Pat Buntrock *have worked in Sarawak for ten years.*

Fingers at Peculiar Angles

Our time in Sarawak was rapidly drawing to a close. In seven weeks we would be leaving the Iban tribe with very little likelihood of ever returning. Several thousand Iban had come to the Lord in the past six years and the young church seemed to be reaching a critical stage. Leaders from their own people seemed the key to their future. Our remaining weeks would be vital.

My wife and I had been concentrating on the development of leaders during our final and very short term among these people. We had come down river eight days before to the small trading post of Pakan where we had a home five or ten minutes walk out in the bush. I had continued on my way to a different river system where I had run five days of training for Christians, while my wife and two of our children stayed at Pakan. During that time Pat had enjoyed many pleasant hours of fellowship with Pastor Tunggi's wife. This couple had become very close to us over the last five years. Together we had prayed and preached, sweated, laughed and cried over the Iban and all that had been needed in initial, grass-roots evangelism among them. Together we had seen the church come to birth, and had nurtured, helped and taught, as the devil fought for ground not rightfully his.

We had also seen this young couple themselves grow tremendously in the Lord. They were of a different tribal group so were missionaries in a very real sense. They had given up a job with far more financial security and nowhere near the demands of this one of planting a church among the Iban. In two days' time they were to leave for a holiday prior to going into Bible school, for in spite of being a fully fledged pastor-evangelist for five years Pastor Tunggi had never had the opportunity of formal study. This was the reason Pat and the two children had come out from the interior, to wish a formal and heartfelt goodbye to these two folk to whom we had become so close.

It was mid morning. Pat had gone into the nearest big town some thirty miles away to stock up our "larder" back up river and have her hair trimmed. I was working on my saw bench, which had a 14″ silicone carbide tipped blade on it. We had been extremely pleased with this, and had only recently had it sharpened for the first time after three years use. It had ripped up countless floor boards and wall boards, including other timbers up to 2″ × 3″. It was a simple affair powered by a 5 HP Honda engine mounted underneath the bench and driving the blade via a vee belt.

At the critical moment I was ripping up an eight foot long board which had been through our planing machine and was now only ⅜″ thick. My idea was to reduce the board into ½″ strips, take them back up river and make a rack in which to stack the dishes, a kind of drainage cum storage rack, in which the rats would not be able to hide.

Halfway along the cut the board "bucked" and jumped a bit due to the lightness of the board being ripped up. I thought, "I'll need to be careful with this," and took the necessary correction while continuing the cut. I was right to the end of the plank when it happened, and I still don't quite know how, except that I must have lost concentration for a moment. I lifted my left hand and almost immediately it caught in the saw blade. There was the most distinctive sound of cracking bones, and pain. I reeled away from the saw bench and took a quick glance at the damage I knew had to be. The bones were showing. The index and middle fingers were at peculiar angles and longer than they had a right to be. Somehow they were still hanging on, praise the Lord!

I grabbed the damaged fingers very firmly with my right hand, ran around the saw bench and switched it off, and started running for the small government clinic on the edge of town. I called out to an Iban pastor who was also at Pakan at the time, "I've cut myself on the engine! Tell my son I've gone to the clinic!"

I knew I had to run. I was aware the damage was fairly extensive, and before too long my system would catch up with the shock and I would be a prime case to faint. I didn't want that to happen before crossing the deep valley on the narrow six inch plank, or indeed half way across. When I reached the bridge I still felt all right, so I didn't hesitate but headed out over the deep little valley. I remember saying "Thanks, Lord" as I got close enough to the end to guess the rest of the way, because I was starting to have misty vision by this time. The effort of climbing a very steep incline soon after the bridge took its toll, and I came to the top with very wobbly knees and a swooning head. However, the rest was straightforward. A concrete path led to the clinic, taking me past government staff living quarters. My strength seemed to be rapidly vanishing as I wobbled, then developed into violent zigzags down the path. I was aware of the hammering of some tradesmen working by the clinic, so I called for help and tried to continue towards them. Two men caught me before I hit the ground, and very quickly had me installed on the emergency bed in the clinic.

Once the dresser peeled my right hand away from the damaged left hand it was clear he could do little but wash the wound and give pain-killing injections.

Praise the Lord the government Toyota land-cruiser was at Pakan and available to take me into Sarikei hospital. Pastor Tunggi had heard the news by this time and he travelled with me, for which I was thankful. Arriving in Sarikei he immediately set out to locate my wife before she returned to Pakan.

Another thing I praise God for was that the doctor on duty was an Iban man so I was able to speak to him in his mother tongue. I am sure the Lord undertook in this, as he finally gave a very honest and frank assessment of the damage and recommended surgery in Singapore.

The Lord's goodness was far from expended, however. Time was fairly important as microsurgery for tendon repair was going to be necessary. But all public transport between Sarikei and Sibu, the nearest airport, had already stopped for the day. Although he was not normally in Sarikei at this time of the week Pastor George Pandang, our Iban team leader, was contacted and he immediately offered to drive me to Sibu, some eighty miles away. In the meantime my wife had also been contacted and I was able to explain what had happened before I left for Sibu. We reached the crossing point over the mighty Rejang river before the ferry stopped running, and the drive on into Sibu was also uneventful, by contrast with my last trip which had resulted in two blown tyres.

The OMF couple working in Sibu had been trying to obtain bookings across to Singapore for me. But as we got there they reminded me that school broke up the next day so all flights were booked out! In face of this the Lord's peace was very real. That night, the first after the accident, I expected really to start "paying for it" as the local anaesthetic wore off. But amazingly (humanly speaking), I had a good night's rest.

In the morning I was given a seat for the first leg of the flight, and at Kuching I was met by airline staff who handled everything, so that I didn't even have to check in in the normal way. An hour after landing at Singapore I had been admitted to hospital. That night, 34 hours after the accident, I was in the operating theatre. Out of the Bornean jungle and into one of the most up-to-date hospitals in Asia in that short time — and with no big company organizing all its resources, just Almighty God and his loving care for a fumbling servant.

At around the time of the accident Pat's uncle was greatly disturbed and felt that we were in some great need, so much so that he made a trunk call over some two thousand kilometers to Pat's mother. His immediate question was, "What's wrong with the Buntrocks? I feel they are in financial need." Needless to say with airfares, hospitalization, surgeons' and anaesthetists' fees followed by physiotherapy, one could say the Lord had given him the right message! Pat's uncle sent a very generous gift which went towards the financial need.

Approximately one week after my accident a letter from my wife arrived. Pat had seen me in hospital at Sarikei and had spoken to the doctor there, who fully expected amputation to be necessary. As Pat travelled back to the trading outpost of Pakan that night, she was deeply concerned and much in prayer. Then, she told me in her letter, it was as if the Lord interrupted her and said, "Relax, don't worry, I've got ten thousand angels watching over Graeme!" She commented, "You didn't know you were as important as that, did you?"

Later my two eldest children passed through Singapore on their way from Australia to join us in Sarawak. Derek shared with me that on the same day as my accident, as far as we could tell, he had had a very vivid dream. He was jolted awake as he clearly saw me running towards him with an agonized look on my face and one very bloodied hand stretched out towards him. It was so vivid and real that he felt he should rebuke the whole incident in the name of the Lord. He was then filled with a need to pray that I would be able to bear the pain. It was some ten to twelve days before he knew anything of what had happened. In fact, I was amazed at the relatively low level of pain I experienced right through. Although urged to do so, I never had to take any painkiller stronger than panadol, and I only took that in anticipation of probable increase in pain. Of course I know that many others were also praying.

It is now one month since the accident. The microsurgery has been entirely successful and movement is returning to the fingers. For all this I praise the Lord.

The events told here took place in 1961. Jim & Doreen Tootill *have now worked in Thailand for almost thirty years.*

The Comfort of the Scriptures

Just before midnight Doreen sat up and glanced first at her watch and then at the family, all sleeping soundly as the large boat glided smoothly down river towards Bangkok. She lay down to sleep again. Suddenly, reaching a branch of the river and encountering a swift cross-current, the boat gave a lurch, spun around and turned completely over on its side.

Doreen and I and our three children, together with two other missionaries Don and Theo, had left our home in Angthong, Central Thailand, earlier that day to attend the OMF conference. The boat normally came along between five and six p.m., but it was well after seven when it appeared around the bend of the river, approaching us rapidly. We waved our torches, the engine slowed down and the boat turned toward us; then suddenly and unaccountably its bell clanged, and it turned away and speeded on to Angthong market.

In consternation I grabbed a bike and raced in pursuit. "Why didn't you stop and pick us up?"

"Sorry, couldn't be bothered; we're mainly carrying goods. But we'll wait for you — we'll be standing here over half an hour."

Quickly I hired a small motor boat and retraced the five minutes up river to bring the whole party back with me. But meanwhile another boat — the usual one — had come, and I returned to find everyone already on board. Clambering on to the upper deck, our family found a suitable place, with Don and Theo on the opposite side. We finished eating our sandwiches, begun while waiting on the river bank, and lay down to sleep.

I woke to the sound of screams, and even as my head jerked round in the direction of the nearby group of terrified women, I saw out of the corner of my eye what appeared to be a huge wave breaking over the boat. Actually it was our side of the boat crashing down into the river, and we were all plunged deeply into the water. We bobbed up to the surface like corks, and despite the darkness were able to grasp the upper side of the boat as it was carried rapidly down stream floating on its side in the middle of the wide river. As Doreen came up through the water her hand brushed against something which she immediately recognized as the baby's dress, and instinctively clutching it she brought Barbara up with her. David, the eldest, appeared and was quickly grasped; but two-and-a-half-year old Janet was missing.

An attempt to plunge into the interior of the boat

seemed to make it heel over dangerously, and had to be abandoned immediately. After some minutes, a small launch came alongside and Doreen, David and Barbara were taken away to the bank. Kindly folk took them into a house to wait, and there Doreen was able to pray with David, mentioning the probability that Janet was already in heaven with the Lord Jesus. David accepted this fact with wonderful calmness, and from then on witnessed concerning it to the Thai.

Meanwhile the big boat floated swiftly on down-river with us three men still clinging to it, hopes diminishing. It was several minutes later that a woman some 25 feet away along the side of the boat called out, "Here's the foreign child — dead." I saw her dress, and in a few moments we had her with us. How grateful we were! Don and Theo commenced valiant efforts at artificial respiration under appalling circumstances, but without success. It seemed clear, from the bruising on one side of her head and body, that while still sleeping Janet was struck by some of the heavy goods piled nearby, and that at some time during the twenty minutes before she appeared our Saviour came and gathered her to Himself.

Soon we were the only ones left on the boat, because the superstitious Thai in the many small crafts dotted all around, having heard the woman's cry, were afraid to receive us. How we longed to get on to dry land, especially when the boat heeled right over again and we scrambled up on to the roof; it was by God's protecting mercy that it didn't sink. Then, as we approached another junction in the river, a small boat came near and finally rescued us. It took us to a jetty where, although it was now one a.m., a crowd of kindly folk soon joined us with lamps and towels. There was even a hot water bottle to use on little Janet's body, and a nurse appeared and gave her an injection, so we were able to feel that everything possible was done for her. During that time the other large boat that we might so easily have travelled on sailed serenely by!

It was at this place that we were, amazingly, able to hire a motor boat to take us to look for Doreen. The nurse and a local man accompanied us, and indeed stayed with us till the morning. It was 2.15 a.m. when we found Doreen. She was so peaceful. And now she knew for certain what she had suspected, that our little Janet was with the Saviour. As we had Janet's body with us it was not possible to enter a house, so after much puzzling we accepted a suggestion that we should go on to the local market town, Sena, which had a clinic. As the boatman was still willing to take us, we moved swiftly off for a further half-hour's journey up-river; the weather was unseasonably warm so in spite of being wet through we were not cold.

We shall never forget the kindness of the people of Sena. From the cheery doctor who rose readily from his bed to receive us — and what a comfort it was to be able to lay the little body in a suitable place, and then sit down in a lighted room and drink some hot tea — to the wife of the "mayor", who in her husband's absence came to seek us out about 6.30 a.m., everyone sought to help and sympathize with us. But as we sat in that clinic waiting for the morning to come, the natural "if onlys" began to flood in upon us. *If only* we'd realized which way the boat had capsized, and searched in this place, and that and the other. *If only* that first big boat had stopped and taken us on board, or the second one had come a trifle later so that we would have boarded the first one at the market. *If only* we'd gone by bus yesterday ... though normally boat is decidedly safer and more direct for that journey. These first two in particular were agonizing and persistent.

Meanwhile a distressing problem was pressing itself upon us: to reach Bangkok we must first get to Ayuthya by boat. The man who had brought us so far was willing to take this long journey under the cover of darkness, but was unable to do so through ignorance of the channels; and once it became light neither he nor any other boatman would dare to take us with Janet's body for fear of his boat being boycotted. From Ayuthya maybe a taxi could be induced to take us, for a price. As we talked this over with the doctor one ray of hope emerged — the American Baptist missionary at Ayuthya, who had paid his weekly visit to Sena just the previous day, had a speedboat.

Before morning came, two principles had begun to register in our minds. First, this thing has happened and cannot be altered, *what matters essentially now is our attitude to it*; and secondly (in the face of feelings otherwise) the *right* thing to do will be to carry on in every way as normally as possible. Perhaps these sound rather cold, but we believe they represented God's guidance to us at that point, and though they didn't come in terms of Scripture, they are well endorsed by I Cor. 15:58 and Acts 20:24.

At six o'clock the doctor led me through the still deserted streets to the post office to see if we could get a phone call through to the missionary in Ayuthya, Mr Spear. On the way he pointed out a shuttered shop as the place they used for their meetings and then, seeing a gleam of light through the cracks, he called out to the occupant. The Thai man who appeared informed us that Mr Spear had remained for the night and was sleeping there! With what relief and gratitude I learned a few moments later that he actually had his own speedboat with him, and that from Ayuthya he would take us on to Bangkok in his volkswagon.

However, our hopes of being on the way in half an hour were disappointed when we learned that the police wished to investigate the circumstances of the accident, and to our dismay this took over two hours. But just before we left they gave us a death certificate, and we discovered later that without this document no burial would have been possible in Bangkok. If we had not been advised to go to Sena, or had left earlier for Ayuthya, we would have been compelled to make the long journey back from Bangkok to obtain that essential document of which we didn't realize our need, and which could only be issued at that place.

So, at 9.30 a.m., cheered by a multitude of kindnesses, we set off down river; peaceful in the knowledge of Janet being in the Heavenly Home, bewildered and distressed by the relentless "if onlys", and with the aim before us to carry on as usual. It was a simple remark made to comfort us by our superintendent's wife, after we had reached Bangkok, that brought light flooding into our hearts. "She was such a precious flower," she said, "and God has transplanted her into His garden."

There was immediate comfort in the sweetness of this thought, but a little while later it caused a question to pose itself: "Could it be that God wanted, and purposely plucked, the flower?" *But of course.* We are His own children and nothing can happen to us outside His will. The Lord in His sovereign purpose gathered our little one to Himself. From the beginning He gave her to us for those two delightful years and eight months. And that evening we understood and could say gratefully, "The Lord gave, and the Lord hath taken away: blessed be the Name of the Lord." Once this fact was grasped, every detail fell into place and a deep peace filled our hearts. The painful "if onlys" were finished, and there was no question of "why?", for we know that "As for God, His way is perfect" and that He has the right to do as He will with His own. All might not be fully understood, but He can certainly be fully trusted. We also sought to embrace His special purpose for ourselves in what had happened.

On the way to Bangkok we had lamented our lack of any recent pictures of Janet. Imagine therefore our delight when we found a whole envelope-full waiting for us. A fellow-missionary who had recently stayed with us had taken several splendid pictures of the children. The beautiful ones of Janet meant so much to us, and were such a token of the Lord's love.

The funeral service was held at eight o'clock the following morning, and our feet were firmly planted on those words, "O Death, where is thy sting? O grave, where is thy victory? ... Thanks be to God, which giveth us the victory through our Lord Jesus Christ." The Scriptures were deeply satisfying to our souls, and we were able to express our response in the words of the hymn, "God moves in a mysterious way."

"Judge not the Lord by feeble sense,
But trust Him for His grace;
Behind a frowning providence
He hides a smiling face.

Blind unbelief is sure to err,
And scan His work in vain;
God is His own interpreter,
And He will make it plain."

Travelling on down to conference a few hours later we marvelled at the fulfilment of the promise, "God is faithful, who will not suffer you to be tempted above that ye are able", for truly we would have imagined that these things were beyond what we could bear. But verse after verse of Scripture came to nourish our hearts: "... that you may prove what is that good, and acceptable, and perfect will of God"; "The God of hope fill you with all joy and peace in believing, that you may abound in hope"; "He hath done all things well"; "Blessed is he, whosoever shall not be offended in Me." And such passages as 2 Cor. 1:3-5, Heb. 12:3-11, and 1 Pet. 1:3-8 came readily to mind and took on new meaning. We sensed something of the opportunity, the responsibility, even the privilege of trusting and glorifying the Lord through such an experience.

Conference was a marvellous provision for us with the loving fellowship of our fellow-workers, and the occupation of mind and heart with the rich ministry of God's Word and with consideration of the work throughout our field. Often we felt like those "made a spectacle unto men", but the peace of God which guarded heart and mind was truly beyond all understanding.

Returning to our home we were overwhelmed with kindly visitors, but it was so hard to tell the story and to answer questions again and again. Many wept, and it was our task to comfort them with the assurance of our Saviour's triumph over death and of Janet's being more alive than ever, and happy with the One Whom she had so much loved to hear and sing about. Then the letters came flooding in, over a hundred of them from all parts, and how strengthening we found them: we marvelled at the accumulation of sorrow and faith in them, representing the truest sympathy. David returned without any fear to sleep in the bedroom he had shared with Janet; though we often noticed how much he missed his playmate, he knew quite clearly that she was safely with the Lord Jesus — what a mercy this was for him!

Left to ourselves Christmas would surely have been a sad time: but 36 of Doreen's students sharing Christmas Eve with us, and 75 children, students and neighbours packing into our back platform on Christmas night and giving wonderful opportunities of recounting the Good News, made it instead a deeply happy time.

As we looked back two months after the fearful event, we realized that we had not been given a "comforting presence" to carry us through, but rather an impregnable rock — the sure Word of God — upon which to plant our feet. We were called to walk by faith. There were many "fiery darts" — a sense of painful loss, the feeling of bewilderment, sometimes a horrifying recollection of the accident, often a desperate longing to see her come running in — but the Shield of Faith could quench them all; and we learned in a new way to wield the Sword of the Spirit. We were sure that God had further purposes to reveal, and we eagerly anticipated that He would bring much blessing to many people out of the seeming tragedy: "He purposeth a crop." It was His perfect will for little Janet for whom all is joy, and for us, and for others; and His grace has proved sufficient for the trial.

"When through the deep waters I call thee
     to go,
The rivers of grief shall not thee overflow;
For I will be with thee, thy trials to bless,
And sanctify to thee thy deepest distress.

When through fiery trials thy pathway
    shall lie,
My grace all sufficient shall be thy supply;
The flame shall not hurt thee, I
    only design
Thy dross to consume, and thy gold
    to refine."

Doug Vavrosky *now works in Taiwan.*

When the windshield crashes in

It was June, 1983, and I was at a friend's house learning to play the guitar. Because of his skill, I stayed at his house until midnight. At this time my thoughts went back to my wife, and the fact that if I didn't get home soon she would wake and be worried about me. Therefore my friend offered to take me home in his car. He lived in an area of the city which was almost entirely surrounded by construction sites; so it was still largely uninhabited, and the number of street lights left much to be desired. As we rode home in his little Honda Civic we were having the most wonderful conversation and, in light of this, we were taking longer to get home than would usually be necessary.

As we were riding along, a motor scooter with two men on it came whizzing past us. They seemed to be travelling at a rather high speed and carrying on rather recklessly, but I thought nothing of it, as it was late and they had probably had a little too much to drink. They drove ahead of us until they were almost out of sight, then I lost interest in them. But behind us I heard another motor scooter which seemed to be deliberately staying behind us for some reason. This didn't worry me either, until I looked ahead once more and saw a man standing in the distance. It was the same man who had been on the back of that reckless motor scooter! As we drew closer to the fellow who stood in the middle of the road, the seriousness of the situation became more and more evident to me, because he was holding in his hand nothing other than a Japanese Samurai sword. This is the traditional fighting weapon of the Bushido, the warrior aristocracy of Japan, and is extremely deadly. It has a handle long enough to grasp with both hands, and a blade from about two and a half to three feet long. It is a heavy weapon, much like a saber, and would have no difficulty in severing a head or a hand with a single swipe.

As we began to slow our car down to a halt, so the two men behind us began to move in on us, and at the same time another scooter approached from our side with two men on it. Each of the passengers on these motor scooters had their own Japanese Samurai swords ready for action. As you can imagine, I didn't really know what to think!

The first thought that came to my mind was that the men were robbers, probably wanting our money or maybe even our car. Well, the car wasn't mine, but my friend would have taken quite a loss. As for money, I probably only had US$50 on me at the very most. My wife's expensive guitar was lying on the back seat, but it would be better to lose that than to lose a head, so from that aspect of it I really had little to fear. My second thought was a bit more frightening. After all I was a foreigner in an Asian country, and "everybody knows how filthy rich those foreigners are." I had been reading in the newspapers lately about the very frequent kidnappings throughout Asia, especially of foreigners. The third thought that came into my mind was that these men were insane, and wanted to get their kicks out of seeing some heads roll. This third possibility was the one I dreaded most, but as we finally wheeled to a stop it was the one that seemed most real.

The moment our wheels stopped their motion, the gangster who had been standing in front of our car began his charge toward us. He lifted his sword, pointed it towards our windshield in typical warrior fashion, and dashed straight for us. My friend and I were quite willing to be robbed, I was even willing to let them take me hostage as a kidnap victim, but this battle charge towards our defenceless little Honda Civic solidified in my mind the fact that more than likely these guys had a mental deficiency. Therefore I yelled at my friend, as he yelled back, "REVERSE!" And off we went down the road, full speed backwards, with a mad gangster holding a Japanese Samurai sword chasing close behind.

As we went flying down the street in reverse, not even able to see where the street behind us led to, we crashed into an American-made Ford LTD. As it was about three times the size of our little car, it suffered little damage, whereas our seats went crashing down and our little Honda jerked to a stop. My friend and I lay on the floorboards, not knowing for an instant who or where we were. The gangsters, however, wasted little time in continuing their attack, and as soon as they reached us they let loose again with Samurai swords flying. I can distinctly remember the glass of the windshield being shattered by the smash of Samurai swords. A sword thrusting inside the car just missed me, and another pierced in on the driver's side under the top part of the steering wheel, so that I thought it was stabbing into my friend as he lay crooked in his seat, still stunned from the accident. The other gangsters were busy smashing out the windows in the back of the car. The swords thrusting in and out were too many even to count. It was evidently a miracle of God's grace that neither of us had so much as a single scratch on us.

At that time I knew without doubt that I would soon be in heaven facing my Lord and Saviour Jesus Christ. My reaction was different from any other time I had come so close to death. Previously fear had gripped me to the point of hysterics. There was the time when I had been set on by thugs in an American city at night. As they approached me with threats and curses, fear gripped me to the point of panic, and I went flying down the city street with suitcase in hand. Another passerby had come to help me, and we escaped on a bus. That incident had frightened me tremendously. But now, as I was face to face with death, I felt absolutely no fear. As the gangsters were beating on our car with their swords, I just committed my spirit to Christ and began praying for my friend, because I knew he still hadn't believed on Jesus Christ as his personal Saviour.

Because the thugs couldn't seem to stab us from inside the car, they decided to drag us out onto the street where they could get a better whack at us. My door, fortunately, had been ruined in the crash and would not open, otherwise that would have been the end of me. My friend had a good strong left arm, and as one of the gangsters tried to pull him out he smashed him in the face, knocking him over. As the gangster went tripping backwards, the car started. I am convinced to this day that it was the Lord who started the car, because my friend was too busy fighting off the gangster to have done it. We immediately drove up a small embankment, chasing one of the gangsters into the countryside. From the top of the embankment my friend somehow manoeuvered the car back onto the road and we were off.

As we were driving away at full speed ahead, which was about half of the original full speed, we had some difficulty staying on the road. This was because the driver had lost his glasses and really couldn't see a whole lot without them. Before the gangsters could come after us in hot pursuit, we managed to ram into the side of a trailer, which just about finished the job the gangsters had started. This gave them a chance to catch up with us.

We were now on a busy road, with many street

lights and people all over, but that didn't stop these fellows who seemed bound and determined to get us. They surrounded our car and used their Samurai swords to direct us over to the side of the road. I was desperately praying for a policeman to come by, but it seemed as if the Lord knew that we didn't need one. My friend stopped the car, jumped out and fell on his knees begging the gangsters to spare his life. I was still stuck inside the car, unable to get out because of my jammed door. But I saw one of the gangsters raise his sword ready to cut my companion's head off, so I quickly prayed. As I was praying I saw the leader of the gang look over in my direction, and his mouth dropped open. He hadn't realized that there was a foreigner in the car!

Immediately two of the other gangsters helped my friend to his feet, and the leader was pulling at my arm through the broken window, shaking my hand wildly, calling me his American friend. After each one of the gang members had had a good look at me, they rode off on their motor scooters to attack some other poor defenseless victims.

Why had they attacked us in the first place? They didn't know us, and we certainly didn't run in their social circles. The possibilities are many; kicks, revenge, mistaken identity, extortion. I believe the real reason is that they were directly controlled by Satan. Some weeks prior to this event I had become involved in a ministry that dealt in a very direct way with sinners where they are, that is, on their way to hell because of their sin! A person cannot talk about sin and judgement without getting people's backs up and, even more so, without getting Satan's back up. Therefore, I believe Satan's reasons for this attack were to see if I really practiced what I preached concerning not being afraid of death and pain, and to nip this ministry in the bud. Up to that point, nobody had come to know Christ as Saviour through that ministry, but since the gang attack at least eight people have accepted Christ, including my friend from that night, and many backslidden Christians have been restored.

When death threatens us we need not fear, for Christ our Risen Lord has gone through death's door before us, and has defeated death's doorkeeper Satan. We need not worry about our reaction at that time, because His grace is certainly sufficient for us in this and every situation, and the peace which surpasses all understanding will certainly be given to us in full measure.

Hudson Taylor, *founder of the China Inland Mission (now OMF) experienced many traumas during his years as a missionary in China. This event took place in 1848.*

Yangchow riot

It was widely known that the deeds for a property in Chinkiang had been signed and the deposit paid. The Governor, however, was withholding the proclamation without which the landlord could not be kept to his bargain, and the whole affair was the laugh of tea-house and restaurant.

Hudson Taylor was carrying on these negotiations from the neighbouring city of Yangchow, where his wife and family and Emily Blatchley were settled in big rambling premises. The place was besieged with visitors at first, and Maria had her hands full. Exaggerated reports about the situation in Chinkiang, however, had suggested to the *literati* that the missionaries might be treated with as scant courtesy in Yangchow. Why allow them to make friends and settle down, when by carrying things with a high hand they could be ejected? A meeting was held and a decision arrived at to stir up trouble. This was done by means of anonymous hand-bills, attributing the most revolting and unnatural crimes to foreigners, especially those whose business it was to propagate "the religion of Jesus."

Early in August, the missionaries began to realize the change that was coming over the attitude of the people. Friendly visitors had given place to crowds of the lowest rabble about the door, and a fresh set of posters was as fuel to the fire.

"On Saturday the 15th," wrote Reid who, with Rudland, had arrived from Nanking, "Mr Taylor received an anonymous letter, advising him to use all possible precautions, as on the following day there was to be a riot. The people assembled at an early hour, and began knocking and battering upon our door until we thought it best to go out and try to pacify them."

The trouble went on, and on the 18th Emily Blatchley wrote: "For the last few days we have been almost in a state of siege. Today (Tuesday) was placarded as the day for attacking our house and setting it on fire, regardless of native or foreign occupants. Once or twice the mob has seemed inclined to break in by force, but the disturbance is less than on Sunday. God is with us, we do not fear. As I write He is sending thunder and the threatening of rain, which will do more for us, Mr Taylor was saying, than an army of soldiers. The Chinese shun rain: the most important matters they will postpone on account of it."

After this, it looked as though the worst was over. In spite of all that had been said against them, the quiet, friendly demeanour of the missionaries was winning its way, and the storm seemed to have spent itself without disaster. From Wednesday to Saturday the wearied household had a little respite, but before the close of the week an opportunity occurred for reviving the agitation. A couple of foreigners from Chinkiang came up to visit Yangchow, and were seen in various parts of the city. This was too good a chance to be lost, and no sooner had they left, with the impression that all was quiet, than reports began to be circulated that children were missing in all directions, entrapped by the "foreign devils." The weather was intensely hot, which always makes for excitable gatherings. Children *had* disappeared, so the people believed — 24 at least had fallen a prey to the dreaded foreigners. And on their premises, as was well known, vast stores of treasures were accumulated! Boatloads of goods had been brought in only a few days previously. Courage! Avenge our wrongs! Attack — destroy! Much plunder shall be ours.

Forty-eight hours later, in a boat nearing Chinkiang, Emily Blatchley's letter was bravely finished:

"We have had to flee from Yangchow. I cannot stop now to describe the last few days, if indeed they are describable. The rioters sacked every room excepting mine, in which were all our most important papers and the bulk of our money — a considerable sum, $300, having reached us from Chinkiang only an hour before the breaking into the house.

"Poor Mr Reid is the most severely hurt of all; a brick-bat struck his eye while he was standing ready to catch Mrs Taylor and me — as we had to escape for our lives by jumping from the verandah roof over the front of the reception hall. Mrs Taylor hurt her leg very much. I, whose fall was not broken (as Mr Reid was wounded, and so disabled from helping me) came down on my back on the stones, and it is only by God's great lovingkindness that I have not a broken spine or skull. I have only a wound on my arm, and that the left arm. It is getting very painful, but there is so much to be thankful for that this seems as nothing."

Murder, though intended, had been averted again and again. Both Taylor, exposed to all the fury of the populace on his way to seek help of the authorities, and those he had to leave in the besieged dwelling, were alike protected by the wonder-working hand of God.

"But for the protection afforded us by the darkness," he wrote of that desperate effort to summon aid, "we should scarcely have reached the *yamen* alive. Alarmed by the yells of the people the gate-keepers were just closing the gates as we approached, but the momentary delay gave time for the crowd to close in upon us; the as yet unbarred gates gave way to the pressure, and we were precipitated into the entrance hall. Had the gates been barred, I am convinced that they would not have been opened for us, and we should have been torn to pieces by the enraged mob.

"Once in the *yamen* we rushed into the judgement hall, crying *Kiu-ming! Kiu-ming!* (save life, save life), a cry the Chinese Mandarin is bound to attend to at any hour of the day or night.

"We were taken to the room of the Chief Secretary, and kept waiting three-quarters of an hour before we had an audience with the Prefect, all the time hearing the yells of the mob a mile or more off, destroying, for aught we knew, not only the property but possibly the lives of those so dear to us. And at last when we did get an audience, it was almost more than we could bear with composure to be asked as to what we really did with the babies; whether it was true we had bought them, and how many; what was the cause of all this rioting? etc.

"At last I told His Excellency that the real cause of all the trouble was his own neglect in not taking measures when the matter was small and manageable; that I must now request him first to take steps to repress the riot and save any of our friends who might still be alive, and afterwards make such inquiries as he might wish, or I would not answer for the result.

"'Ah,' he said, 'very true, very true! First quiet the people and then inquire. Sit still, and I will go to see what can be done.'

"He went out telling us to remain, as the only chance of his effecting anything depended on our keeping out of sight; for by this time the number of rioters amounted to eight or ten thousand.

"We were kept in this torture of suspense for two hours, when the Prefect returned with the Governor of the military forces of the city and told us that all was quiet; that the Governor himself, the captain of the soldiers who guard the gates, and two local Mandarins had been to the scene of the disturbance;

that they had seized several of those who were plundering the premises, and would have them punished. He then sent for chairs, and we returned under escort.

"When we reached the house, the scene was such as baffled description. A pile of half-burned reeds showed where one of the attempts to fire the premises had been made; strewn about everywhere were the remains of boxes and furniture broken and smouldering — but no trace of inhabitants within."

After a long and agonizing search it was with unspeakable thankfulness he learned that some at any rate of the party were hiding in a neighbour's house. The darkness of the night had favoured their escape from their own burning premises. Taken from one room to another as the danger of discovery increased, they had finally been left without a glimmer of light in the innermost apartments.

"Mr Reid lay groaning with pain," wrote Emily Blatchley of this ordeal, "the poor tired children wanted to sleep and we dared not let them, as at any moment we might have to flee again. Mrs Taylor was almost fainting from loss of blood; and I now found that my arm was bleeding from a bad cut, and so painful that I could not move it, while most of us were stiff and sore with bruises."

Then it was the suspense about Taylor and Duncan was hardest to bear. In the darkness and silence, the uncertainty was terrible.

"I cannot attempt to describe to you our feelings," Maria wrote. "But God was our stay, and He forsook us not. This confidence He gave me, that

He would surely work good for China out of our deep distress.

"At last, after a much shorter time than it appeared to us, we heard my husband's voice outside the door, which had been barred for greater safety. He told us that the rioters had all been driven out, and he thought we might venture back to our own rooms, for there would be a guard around the premises. How our hearts went up to God in thanksgiving that He had spared us to each other!

"For the remainder of the night we were in quiet, though for some of us there was no sleep. Early in the morning the guard retired, and the people began to come in again to plunder. Again my husband had to go to the *yamen*, and again commenced a season of anxiety similar to, though in some respects more trying, than the night before. Once more my room became our sanctuary, till just when it seemed as if in another minute the crowd would be upstairs, the alarm was given that the Mandarin had come, and his soldiery soon dispersed the people."

It was *thankfulness* more than anything else that filled the hearts of that little company, wounded and suffering as they were, on the boats that took them to Chinkiang. The Mandarins had insisted on their leaving for a time, that the house might be repaired and the people quietened; and with no thought of compensation, still less of revenge, the missionaries looked forward to a speedy return. Homeless and despoiled of almost everything, they rejoiced in having being counted worthy to suffer "for the sake of the Name," and their hearts were cheered as they recalled the protecting care of God. Their lives had been spared by a miracle and even the money and more important Mission papers were safe, though the room in which they lay had been open to the rioters.[1]

[1] Adapted from pages 293-298 of *The Biography of James Hudson Taylor*, by Dr & Mrs Howard Taylor (Hodder & Stoughton).

The story of Nick & Raili Watkins' *marriage and call to OMF is told in* When God Guides. *They have been working in the Philippines since 1980.*

All my tears ...

"Daddy, who's that?"

"That's Matthew. He's your brother, David."

"Daddy, where's Matthew?"

"Matthew is with Jesus in heaven ..."

Satisfied for the moment, David turned the pages of the photo album to find some other pictures. He is still a bit too young to understand what happened to his brother. Perhaps when he is a little older we will be able to tell him more.

Matthew was born a year before David, but David never saw him because Matthew died at the age of only five weeks. As I write this, four years have elapsed since his death and God has given us two more lovely boys to fill our hearts with joy. Nonetheless the day that Matthew died still remains vividly imprinted on our minds. It marked for us the greatest turmoil that we have yet experienced in our lives.

The shock of finding him dead in his pram left us numb. It was as if we suddenly took a step back from reality and receded into ourselves. Looking back, I can only describe it as being like watching what was going on around us on a television screen. We were somehow not quite there. The interview with the police was performed mechanically. For a while I could not grasp what had happened, and my tears only started to roll when my Dad arrived. I just flung myself into his arms and wept. The ambulance men reminded me of my responsibility to help my wife. "Men usually take it better," they commented, trying to be helpful. In a way it was true. Although I felt numbed by what had happened I forced myself to step back into reality to try and comfort Raili.

If the shock of the first day left me numb and Raili inconsolable, the days and nights that followed were not much of an improvement. We did little during the day but sit in my parents' front room, talk, cry and drink tea. The nights were just as miserable, with sleep often eluding us or bad dreams haunting Raili.

Almost immediately, however, we found that we had more than one foe to fight. As if it wasn't enough to wrestle with grief, guilt also raised its ugly head. The coroner reported the cause of death as "Sudden Infant Death Syndrome," also known as cot death. In effect he was saying that the cause of Matthew's death was unknown, outside the realm of medical knowledge.

This verdict left the door open for us to imagine all sorts of reasons for Matthew's death, nearly all of them attributable to our negligence. For me the period of self blame was only a few days; for Raili the guilt feelings lasted well over a year and still occasionally cause her trouble today. Time and time again we would go over the events preceding Matthew's death, scrutinizing each detail, and inevitably Raili would come to the conclusion that she was to blame. In my anguish and grief I would try and reason her out of her illogical conclusions, until finally something would snap and I would get angry with her.

I have no doubt that our marriage was under considerable strain at that time. Marriages have been known to break up under the strains of Sudden Infant Death. We tried all sorts of remedies to ease the tension. We visited a doctor whom we trusted and Raili shared with him her guilt feelings. Since he was not only a physician but a brother in the Lord, he was able to give us helpful advice, and his reassurances concerning Sudden Infant Death helped Raili considerably. Nevertheless guilt feelings continued to bother her, and I proved more of a hindrance than a help. Sometimes when I felt I was in danger of losing my temper I would send Raili to visit a Christian friend who lived only a few blocks away. "Go and see Linda," was a phrase I used more than once during those difficult times. When my patience was coming to an end Linda would take over and give some of her precious time to listening to Raili.

The road to recovery was long and difficult, with many setbacks. However, there are some milestones that clearly stand out along the way. One was an

OMF conference we attended in Wales. We're not quite sure why Raili started thinking along these lines, but midway through the conference she shared with me: "Just suppose I was guilty, isn't it true that the blood of Jesus is able to take away every sin?" Her reasoning was sound and it seemed to us that God was indeed speaking to us.

Meanwhile God was also applying His balm to my wounds. Although I did not suffer from guilt, my grief was nonetheless real. I had loved Matthew too, and I felt completely alone in my grief. Raili could not help me very much, she had her own battle to fight. Who then would comfort me? Sometimes when I felt pierced by grief I could do no more than weep in the presence of God. Words just didn't come. But if words failed God did not. During those times of weeping in God's presence I felt as if God was holding me in his arms. I knew for certain that God cared. As David put it, I knew that all my tears were stored in His bottle (Psalm 56:8).

The book of Job also became very meaningful to me, answering one big problem that had been bothering me. Had God taken Matthew because he was angry or displeased with us? Was this disaster in fact a kind of punishment or sign of God's disapproval? Job's experience suddenly began to make sense. Job had not suffered because God was displeased with him — quite the contrary. God had allowed Job to suffer because He loved him. In Job's case his suffering was a sign of God's approval. So too I believe (though I don't understand) that God took Matthew not because he hated us but because he loved us and approved of us. In the midst of intense grief there was assurance of God's love. This poem was written shortly after Matthew died:

> O Lord he was my son
>> he was my son
> We had great plans for him
> We remember the day he was born
>>> the time he sat upon my knee
>>> the look he gave his Mum
>>> the words he tried to make but
>>> never came
> He had a lot to say but no words to say with
> O Lord he was our son
>> our first born son
> We were proud of him
> We loved him
> But now O Lord You have taken him
>> and his parents' arms are empty
>> and their bodies ache for him
> But Matthew is with You Lord
> O Lord hear our prayer
>> for we are heart broken
> Fill our lives again
> You have stored all our tears in Your wineskin
> You see that Your servants need You now
> Was it because You were angry with us
>> that You did this?
>> that You smashed our hopes?
> No! it was because You loved us and approved
>> of us that You let this happen
> Lord, look after our son. We know You will.

This story would not be complete without reference to David's birth, another milestone along the path of healing. David was born in Singapore. We had only just arrived in Asia to begin our missionary service and were attending the OMF Orientation Course. I had the privilege of being present in the delivery room when David made his noisy entrance into the world, and two things were immediately obvious: he was a boy and he was healthy. We were overjoyed. Raili had been like Hannah, beseeching God to give her a son. Now we held God's answer in our arms. It was as if light and life had again entered our lives after the long months of darkness.

Yet in the midst of our joy we faced another crisis. Matthew had died at the age of five weeks. Would David survive the early weeks of life? As the five-week mark approached we felt more and more anxious, and Raili hardly slept. Every few minutes she would get up to check that David was still breathing. However, the five-week mark passed uneventfully and we began to relax. For long months Raili had felt far away from God, and prayer had been difficult. David's arrival changed all that. She began to talk to God, and God's Word again spoke to her. David's birth had brought new life in more ways than one.

God has done much healing in our lives, and yet we still have to say the healing is not complete. Even so long after the event pain still pierces our hearts. Sometimes a remark or an event will bring back memories of Matthew, making us yet again yearn for him. In the legend of King Arthur, the fatally wounded King is taken across the waters to an island where his wounds would find healing. In a similar way, I believe we need to cross over to that place of healing written about in God's Word. Only in that place where death and crying are no more will the last tear be wiped away from our eyes.

Gill Stedeford *and her husband James work in East Malaysia.*

Where is God when it hurts?

At first we thought James had a migraine due to working too long in the sun. He had joined the workparty painting the outside of the wooden church in preparation for our church conference in Lawas, Sarawak, and then after lunch he hammered planks together and made crates for the trunks which would store our belongings during furlough. Our flight back to England was booked for 4th December and it was already Wednesday 27th October. Time was precious, as James was going away for three weeks with the Bible School students on their practical work.

Next day James couldn't get up, and it hurt him to lift his head from the pillow. Helen and Peter were not allowed to play in their bedroom, adjoining ours, because of Daddy's headache. All Friday too he stayed in bed, getting up in the evening to shower but struggling back to bed again afterwards. The students had prepared an end-of-year cele-bration for that evening and the children, dressed in their best, went to the party care of "Auntie" Mary. We ate some of the chicken and rice that the students handed in to us, but James had not eaten for nearly two days and didn't want much.

Together with some of the Ladies Fellowship I had planned to visit a neighbouring village church the next day. Now I didn't know whether I should leave him. James thought he would be all right, and encouraged me to go. We prayed about it, then slept.

A heavy thud woke me. James had fallen out of bed and lay writhing on the floor, his body jerking. His breath came in laboured gasps and his swollen face showed no recognition of me. I thought he was going to die there and then, and cried out to God for help. "Please God, don't let him die!" I muttered. "Please God, don't let him die." Suddenly two small white-faced figures appeared in the doorway. I brought the children over and we prayed together. James was not shaking so much now. I got him a pillow.

"Stay here with Daddy, Helen," I told her. "I must fetch Uncle Julian." Surprisingly, Helen didn't object. I picked up Peter and the torch, found my way into our neighbour's house and banged on their bedroom door.

"Julian!" I yelled. "James is very sick, we'll have to get him to the hospital."

A startled Julian responded. Then we stumbled across the grass to the Belchers' house, and I shouted up to Alan who came immediately. It seemed ages before a stretcher appeared, and light was streaking the sky as we left the house. Various neighbours had gathered in our front room by this time. Helen and Peter went next door to Alau, Julian's wife, and I promised I would be back to see them later. Our close friend Kingas wept as I hurried to catch up the makeshift stretcher. Somehow we got across the river in a small boat, and into the waiting ambulance. James' eyes were open and I told him what was happening, but he didn't seem to be registering much.

After a short ambulance ride we arrived at the hospital, still quiet at six a.m. Orderlies shunted James into a bed while a nurse took details from me, and a lady from the other ward wandered up to see what was happening. Suddenly, horrified, I saw the look in James' eyes change and his face begin to twitch. "Quick, he's having another fit!" I called out. The staff nurse called for oxygen and exclaimed impatiently as the cylinder jammed. She stuck the tube in his nose and injected him with valium.

"In the name of Jesus, in the name of Jesus, we have the victory!" I sang as I tried to control James' shaking body.

"He'll be all right now," a voice said coolly, and the violent shaking stopped as the sedative took effect. I had to go over what had happened again to the young Chinese doctor, who seemed quite unperturbed. "It sounds like viral meningitis," he said, "but we will take tests to make sure."

Saturday outpatients filled the corridor as James was wheeled into the x-ray department, and grave-faced friends from our SIB (Evangelical Church of

Borneo) community stood outside. I had to explain several times over as much as I knew.

Nothing malign showed up in the x-ray so the treatment for viral meningitis was begun. A nurse fixed the saline drip into James' arm, and every six hours she would inject antibiotic solution into the tube. More SIB friends came, and someone brought me coffee and steamed rolls. I was glad of the coffee.

Later that morning James surfaced and seemed fully conscious. I explained where he was.

"I thought you were going to die," I said, and asked his forgiveness for some pettiness of the previous day — I can't remember now what it was.

"Of course I forgive you," he replied.

Just after midday I went back home across the river to see the children. No problems there. The Belchers called and Madge told me, "I think he's on the mend now." After a shower I returned to the hospital, to find two Chinese Christian friends, Dennis and Julia, on the hospital veranda. Julia started to weep and I lent her a big handkerchief, assuring her, "James is getting better now, the treatment has begun."

But once back in the ward some of my assurance vanished. James was conscious and talking — but talking gibberish! He was frowning in his anxiety to communicate, but I couldn't understand anything he was trying to say. He shook his head in his distress at not being able to speak coherently. I felt completely inadequate. "Don't try to talk," was all I could say. "Don't worry," I kept repeating, "just rest."

That night the students from the Bible School took turns to nurse James while I slept on the empty bed beside him, for local custom is that relatives of those seriously ill are expected to stay and help nurse the patients. About 4.30 a.m. I woke and told the students that I could cope now ... but I must have dozed off again, because James fell out of bed trying to get out to go to the toilet. He wrenched out the drip and banged the side of his head, and whimpered pitifully as we heaved him back into bed. I felt awful. I should have been watching, but had fallen asleep!

"Perhaps the knock has disturbed his brain more," I worried.

Later, after I had confessed my negligence to three lady students, one of them arranged for James' bed to be moved to the end of the ward, where only the glass partition separated us from the staff nurse. I also told the doctor that the valium didn't stop James fretting, and he prescribed a stronger sedative which knocked him right out. He was away from us now.

Sunday morning was quiet, but that afternoon many neighbours came in small groups, wanting to pray for James. I was touched by their concern. Dennis and Julia came again, and Julia said, "God wants me to share about the man who fell out of the window." I knew she meant Eutychus, restored to life by Paul ... but I was concerned about James' condition. The fever was not lessening as fast as the doctor had expected. That evening several of the church deacons had gathered round his bed and I asked them to anoint him with oil and pray for his healing. A sympathetic orderly produced some kind of oil and we prayed together.

That night two close friends came to sit with me and help nurse James. His temperature reached 103°, and we sponged his hot body and tried to ease his restlessness. Sometimes I dozed.

About midnight a youth was pushed into the nurses' room by some nervous friends. Every few minutes he would cough and spit, and after questioning by the nurse we discovered he had swallowed a potent weedkiller in a suicide attempt.

"Lord, I don't have faith to pray for his healing," I thought.

Over the following eight days our visitors sometimes prayed with him that the Lord would forgive and accept him. He knew something of Christianity and had a kind of faith. During these long days his skin turned yellow as he tried to spit out the poison that was rotting his stomach. His bewildered parents and sister several times tried to take him away, against medical advice. He must have died shortly afterwards. I shall never forget that pathetic family, though I have forgotten his name. Rejected by his girlfriend, he took his own life and regretted his action too late. No one had given him enough hope to carry on living.

On Monday morning we were encouraged to find James' temperature had come down two degrees, though he was still unconscious due to the sedative. While a friend waited by his bedside I slipped out for a while, and as we sat drinking tea in a nearby cafe I asked Alan Belcher whether he thought I should phone our families in England. Alan suggested waiting, but I was concerned that James' parents at any rate ought to know, in case he died. So later in the day I tried to contact them. The telephone connection took ages, and I left another missionary trying to get through because I didn't want to be away from the hospital too long.

Later that afternoon our Deputy Director Tony Horsfall came to the hospital with me. Tony asked James to squeeze his hand, but there was little response. Probably we shouldn't have expected it, due to the heavy sedation, but at the time I wasn't thinking logically and I went down into the depths. Outside in the corridor I sobbed and sobbed, a delayed reaction to all that had happened. I confessed to God my possessiveness concerning James, and the resentment I felt when he went away leaving me at home with the children. As I cried I gave James back to God for His will, promising that if he recovered I would not hold him back from God's service. I remembered words I had read a month before in the book of Job, "Though he slay me, yet will I hope in him."

As I wept friends stood by me, but I had to open my heart to God regardless of their presence. Tony counselled me not to blame myself for wrong attitudes in the past. "Think positively," he said. "So often we get into a negative way of thinking which is not God's way." He was right. I was already seeing myself on the plane travelling back to England, a widow with two young children. I felt loved and comforted as Dayang, a wise Christian mother from the SIB, took me in her arms and wept with me.

Next morning I was able to be more positive. James' temperature was still erratic but its trend was generally downwards. Tony phoned to find out how things were and to say that we had been too negative the previous day. He had prayed with the Belchers and they had been assured that James would get well. I went to the hairdressers, not wanting James to see me looking a wreck when he came round! A kind-hearted Christian nurse was bringing me a rice meal twice a day, and the locker was embarrassingly full of tinned fruit, milk, meat and biscuits.

Early on Wednesday morning James came to semi-consciousness. The efficient night nurse gestured towards me and asked, "Do you recognize her?" James smiled and said, "Yes." I smiled back, my eyes rather "soggy" as Peter puts it.

After that it was a long slow haul back to full health. James spent our last month in Lawas in enforced rest, frustrated that he could not help me pack. After dark the grasshopper-like cicadas would start up their chain-saw whine on the tree outside our bedroom, and the noise upset James. So the children and I prayed together and asked God to make the cicadas stop. Amazingly, after a minute or two they did.

Arriving in England was wonderful. We tried to explain to our families that God had healed James through prayer. I don't believe that James' healing was a miracle in the same way that the healings of Jesus were; but I do believe that God caused the healing through the timing of events, some of which were in response to prayer. Earlier on, in discussion with the doctor as to whether James should be moved by plane to a larger hospital in Miri, I had said, "I have faith in you, Doctor," and then corrected myself, "No, first of all I have faith in God, and then I have faith in you." That doctor was not a Christian, but God used his medical skill.

I don't know why God allowed this illness to happen. It didn't occur to me then to ask why it happened, although I'm sure if James had died I would still be asking the question. Sickness is part of our fallen world from which Christians are not immune. During James' illness we experienced so much of God's love expressed through the local Christians. Helen, Peter and I saw that God answers prayer. I don't want to belittle the agony when prayer for healing meets with a "No" answer, for we were privileged to hear God's "Yes." Where is God when it hurts? He is with us then too.

Dorothy Beavan, *from New Zealand, has worked in Japan for 23 years.*

Be Still

Stopped at red traffic lights late one night in the Japanese city where I lived, I had not been alarmed to see in my rear-vision mirror the lights of an approaching car, for at such times one expects other traffic to approach. But one also expects them to stop! It was the sound of glass falling around my head, following a jolt and a thud, which alerted me to the fact that I was in a prone position.

Still bound securely by my seat belt, I came back to a more upright position when my groping fingers found the right lever. Inclination made me want to survey the damage, and I had put my hand out through the open window to give myself more leverage before my mind asserted some sort of control. "No, I'd better not try to move any more. There's been an accident, and even if I'm not hurt I'm bound to be suffering from shock. Be still."

The Holy Spirit, in control of our every situation,

so jogged my memory at that point that my line of thought continued naturally, "Be still ... and know that I am God."[1]

How often, in retrospect, have I marvelled at the absence of panic, and at the calm way I accepted what little I knew of the situation. This I can attribute only to the grace of God. To have worried about the extent of the damage to my car and the probable size of repair bills would have been a reaction more normal for me, but instead this timely reminder of God's Word brought with it an indescribable sense of peace, with the knowledge that God was in control.

I realized that I had driven only seven kilometres since filling up with petrol. Yet there had been no explosion, no fire. Presumably the electrical system had been affected with the smashing of the rear lights, and yet I had felt no shock when my hand contacted the metal work beyond the open window. Recalling the sound of broken glass, I investigated cautiously with my fingers. Not only did I appear to have escaped cuts, but I had failed also to bring up fragments of glass when I levered the seat back into position. I was conscious immediately of the miracles of the Lord's protection, and can remember only a deep sense of thankfulness for the ways in which He had proved Himself to be in control. Then, when my mind began to acknowledge more of the facts of the accident, I was able to praise Him for preventing panic and giving peace.

Psalm 46:10

Hearing nothing of the blaring sirens which always herald the arrival of the police, I was surprised when I opened my eyes to see officials examining a man who turned out to be the driver of the four-ton truck which had crashed into me. Although there was good moonlight, the headlights of many police vehicles provided illumination converging on the seat of a motor-cycle which was doing duty as a table. It did occur to me that the driver had had plenty of time in which to concoct a plausible story, and I realized what sort of treatment I, a foreigner and a woman, could expect. But I felt completely indifferent. The Lord gave such peace that I accepted unconcernedly the fact that probably I would be held to blame.

An officer came to demand various documents, obligingly retrieving them from the floor. "Just keep still", was his order as he took them to his makeshift table. "And know that I am God" prompted the Holy Spirit, as I closed my eyes once more, content to await developments. It was not until considerably later that I realized how much effort would have been wasted had I been concerned about my statement to the police. For, when the requirements of the law had been satisfied, about ninety minutes after the accident, the officer returned my documents and turned his attention to my physical condition, informing me that he had sent for an ambulance. Not one single question had he asked me, neither had I been required to make a statement.

The assurance that God was in control more than drove worry from my mind: apparently it interfered with my normal thought processes. The threat of having to go to hospital in an ambulance appalled me. I wanted only to be left in peace to go to sleep. It had not occurred to me that to remain inside a wrecked car in the early hours of Sunday morning was hardly ideal! But common sense agreed with police reasoning, and I acknowledged my need to be seen by a doctor.

"Then please contact Kano hospital," I requested.

"Kano? Where's that?"

Before I could explain, the voice of another policeman broke in: "That's out in Kaneko, beyond the city boundary. No, I'm sorry, but you'll have to go to a city hospital."

By this time I think I was becoming aware that I was not reacting in character. For the past eleven years I had been working among nurses all over Japan, and I knew a lot about Japanese hospitals. I had determined long ago never to be hospitalized in Japan! Later on, after meeting Dr Kano and his nurses, I had been prepared to make an exception, feeling that in an emergency I might be willing to go to the Kano Christian Hospital. But now permission had been refused — and yet I was content!

"The ambulance will be here soon," I was told. "Be still ...."

"... and know that I am God. I have everything under My control, including the matter of hospitalization." How graciously the Lord stilled the potential storms in my heart, flooding my whole being with such an indescribable sense of peace that I was conscious of no pain.

Unable to locate a bed for me, the intern on duty at the Emergency Centre radioed for the ambulance to deliver me there, and I was deposited on the step and left to stagger in. I was still standing at the desk, providing the nurse with information essential to her records, when Dr and Mrs Oka hurried in. It was their home I had left almost two hours earlier, and theirs had been the only phone number I could call to mind on the demand of the police.

"Why didn't you go to Kano?" Mrs Oka wanted to know, marching me to a bed, while the already harrassed intern gazed in awe at the eminent Ear, Nose and Throat Surgeon. The problem of Kano's location was solved when Dr Oka phoned Dr Kano and then signed his responsibility for the action. With police approval the Okas assisted me into their car and headed for Kano, passing within fifty metres of my house en route. The overnight bag which I had unloaded only hours before on my return from Tokyo was still just inside the door, not yet unpacked, and Mrs Oka collected it for me with scarcely a moment's delay. Her "keep still" as I handed over the key was yet another reminder that the Lord had control over every detail.

After taking x-rays and giving me a quick examination Dr Kano announced that he could find nothing broken, but that I must remain overnight. Since it was by now well after two a.m., I found this suggestion palatable enough, although I took literally his "one night."

In the hospital waiting room I found the truck driver, who had been sent by the police to learn the initial verdict. "Please make sure you recover properly," he said, fingering his cap nervously. "And don't worry about the expense. My company's insurance will cover all medical costs." Hearing that, I realized that the police were not holding me to blame, and next day I learned that in fact one hundred percent blame had been allocated against the truck driver — an event so rare that it "never happens"!

As I was assisted up the stairs, little guessing how long it would be before I would walk again, I felt remarkably happy. Oh yes, there had been an accident, and my good car was now a write-off, but I was still alive, I had no wounds — not even scratches — and I had broken nothing. I had been protected from fire and electrocution. Because I had unloaded everything from the car on my return from Tokyo, no additional possessions had been damaged. In all the accidents of which I had heard in which foreigners were involved, they had been held to blame; and yet the other driver had been held at fault, and one hundred percent at fault at that. And, to cap it all, even though the accident had happened within the city limits, I was on my way to bed at Kano, among Christian friends, in the hospital I rated number one in Japan!

"Be still!" said Dr Kano when he came to give me an injection.

"Be still ... and know ... and rejoice ... that I am God."

The fact of the Lord's protection became even clearer when, in an identical accident ten days later, all three in the car were killed outright, their necks broken. The meaning of the phrase translated "killer whiplash" became clearer to me. The general concensus of opinion of the many doctors who examined me seemed to be that I had no right to be alive. According to their reckoning, no one survived such severe whiplash injuries.

Memory becomes blurred after that. The effects of shock, severe whiplash, concussion and weeks of high temperatures led to a total of 370 days of hospitalization. Throughout those days the evidences of the Lord's provision were many. A luxury suite, with refrigerator and colour TV, as well as bathroom, in a Christian hospital, owned and staffed by friends who had visited my house and knew where to find my possessions as I needed them; church friends who anticipated so many of my needs; grand fellowship with nurses who even gave up precious off-duty hours to hold a Christmas party in my room; and all medical expenses met, something in excess of US$27,000, as well as the equivalent of my remittance from the mission also paid, according to Japanese practice, by the insurance company. This happened only because of that "hundred percent" decision. Greatest of all was the special provision of the Lord's peace, which enabled me to face each day as it came, appreciating the concern of nurses and friends, being conscious of the prayers on my behalf and grateful for them in increasingly deeper ways, experiencing the reality of the sufficiency of God's grace for me.

Many friends queried why the Lord had allowed

the accident but, because He had proved so clearly all along that He was in control, I do not remember having any such query in my own mind. It was enough to know that he was in control, and it was thrilling to experience the intimacy of His care.

"What of the future?" was another frequent question, but I saw no reason to think in terms of a future in New Zealand until the Lord had made it clear that the remarkable degree of recovery was still not sufficient to allow me to return to Japan. By that time, opportunities for helping as able with a new venture, a local Christian FM Radio Station, had opened up, and although I must still attend hospital for treatment three days a week I am finding this involvement challenging and satisfying. It is indeed different from my work among Japanese nurses, but while I was in hospital I saw the nurses themselves beginning to develop initiative at last, in ways which would not have happened had I been active.

The accident and its aftermath are not things which I would want to experience again, but I can and do praise God for everything which He saw fit to allow. I am grateful for all that He taught me then of His sovereign power, of His deep concern for the minutest details of my life, and of the importance which He attaches to prayer. It was a time when I stayed still, to watch Him at work, and when I proved His peace to be more than sufficient for my every need, as I know it will continue to be in the days ahead.

Lois Michell *and her husband Brian have worked in Indonesia, Singapore and Malaysia.*

"Cave-In"

I knew when my roof was going to cave in: August seventeenth. But knowing when it is going to happen does not necessarily mean you are in a position to protect yourself from the falling rubble. So the new Chefoo School term saw me slipping down the hill on the ruins of the mother role which had been my chief responsibility since we acquired two babies in one year on our first furlough.

I thought Loretta's troubles a bit farfetched, borrowed from years ahead, when she confided that she had been in tears the day her son was born at the thought of sending him away to school. Five years later, when we received our own new son, I could no longer share my own humour at the tale. The point of it had come right into our own home.

Brian and I believed the Lord wanted us to have a family but after eight years of marriage, when much advice and many investigations had produced no children, it seemed logical and right to adopt a baby. In those days in New Zealand, once the paperwork was completed you could wait two years and more for a baby, so we were shocked only two months later to be told they had a baby for us. In fact I was temporarily horrified. There had been no time to attend any "how to handle the new baby" classes. Jonathan's layette comprised one half-knitted woollen vest! And I don't suppose I had changed a baby's nappies twice in my life.

We learnt very fast. In fact between them Jonathan and David, born to us ten months later as everyone predicted he would be, gave us a crash course in infant welfare. Living miles from home with no competent mothers to advise, rescue or babysit for us we were forced to cope on our own and thus developed a very strong, self-sufficient nuclear family. This was reinforced six months later back on the job in Indonesia where we taught in Satya Wacana Christian University, by our decision that I would care for the boys myself with plenty of help and support from Brian. The normal Indo-nesian practice, by contrast, would be for the mother to go back to work and hand the babies over to a nursemaid whose personality and values would inevitably imprint themselves on the children at a very receptive stage.

This was great for the boys, bearable (I hope) for Brian, but a disastrous dislocation for me. While I was not a rabid career woman, I had worked outside the home in the eight years we had together before Jonathan arrived, so it was a severe shock to be incarcerated in the house with two tiny children. There was nowhere much to take them when we did go out, and certainly nowhere where Jonathan's auburn hair and David's petite charm did not assure us an attentive following. Friends from various missions lived in the town and their homes were blessedly open to us at the five o'clock nadir of the day, but they did present me with a peculiar problem. Mostly their youngest children were half a dozen years older than ours and their mothers had long since forgotten the trials of wakeful nights, potty training and infant ills. I got the impression that none of my friends had experienced my kind of juvenile trials or had failed to cope competently with them. I was the only dumb mama on the block!

This was also the first time Brian's and my paths had diverged. He continued in the teaching role I too had loved and was also appointed to an OMF superintendent-type role for our region, a job which took him away from home every few weeks on the notorious Indonesian night buses. My self-confidence nosedived and shattered on impact.

Into such a stressful situation came two books which made a very basic change, picked me up and put me together again and started me up the ladder once more, not fast but at least up. One was *Ms Means Myself* by Gladys Hunt, which brought home to me how God had chosen to make me with just the personality and abilities he wanted me to have. He accepted me. How could I therefore reject or despise what God accepted and highly valued? The second very practical book, Tim LaHaye's *Spirit-Controlled Temperament*, written in an absorbable form suited to the atrophied mental processes of a mother of small children, stimulated and encouraged me to understand my own personality, appreciating its strengths as well as recognising its weaknesses (much the easier task), and provided resources for change.

Gradually, of course, the crisis of self-confidence lessened, the "little tackers" grew older, we began to revive and grasp our lifestyle and became quite creative in providing educational toys and activities for the boys: plywood manipulative puzzles, a bamboo jungle gym with a slide into the paddling pool, a family-sized tiptruck. By the time Jonathan and David were three and two they formed an imaginative and self-contained play unit and we were writing our friends to stop sympathizing with us for having two children so close together. We discovered we were now on the win.

So we got our act together. I took up some teaching again, enough to keep me sanely stimulated but not overcommitted since I still regarded my home role as the priority one. We painted the house, remade the garden, gained many new friends — and were asked to move along.

For some time we had been praying about moving to one of the outer islands of Indonesia, so understaffed by church workers compared with overpopulated Java, but we were startled to find the Lord taking us up on our prayers further than we had envisaged, to the "outer island" of Borneo, on the Malaysian side of the border.

The "ten year ruling" in Malaysia — a maximum

stay of one decade for expatriates — meant the Borneo Evangelical Mission, now formally merged with OMF, faced losing its leadership. Looking around for someone suitable and available to replace Director Bill Hawes, they asked us to move across. We agreed, though not without immense apprehension on my town-bred part, as the Evangelical Church of Borneo initially proposed to station our little family at Namaus Bible School in Sabah for experience and orientation. The Director's wife advised us to imagine the worst about Namaus in the hope of being pleasantly surprised by actuality. Since she also assured us there were no reliable supplies of meat, vegetables or fruit, no regular transport to the nearest town, no electricity, water supply or househelp, I could not imagine what was left to be "pleasantly surprised" by. The view, perhaps, as I scrubbed my kids and thirty nappies a day in the local stream.

Happily our commitment to this spot in the outer islands was never put to the test, for Immigration would not give us a visa. We received all the credit for being willing to move without having to put our bodies where our brave words were! Eventually we transferred to the oil town of Miri in the neighbour state of Sarawak for Brian to become Area Director of OMF work, initially in the East and subsequently for all Malaysia. In Miri I learned by practising that most nebulous of roles, the Area Director's wife. I back-stopped for Brian, helping his then inexperienced office staff when he was off on his pastoral and church liaison travels; I entertained droppers-in; I experienced an involuntary weight-watchers' course over learning to handle the big station wagon; I taught the boys by correspondence schooling.

"What are you going to do about their schooling?" friend after friend asked with an eye on our lively pair. Jonathan and David were only three and four when we moved to Malaysia and we refused to be panicked into premature decisions. Three choices existed: teach them myself; put them in a local school; or send them to Chefoo, OMF's primary school for its missionaries' children situated in the Cameron Highlands of Peninsular Malaysia. Local kindergarten was fine for their social needs, but educationally it was a washout; the pupils used their reading books for paper darts. But in any case primary schools were switching from English to Malay medium. We were a year behind the change and our boys did not speak Malay. As far as Chefoo was concerned, because of the way our furlough would work out we faced sending Jonathan either for a year and a half when he was very young and immature, or for one term only with all the extra adjustments of furlough to follow.

Teaching did not scare me; I was a teacher although never of small children. The Lord made it obvious that correspondence schooling was His pattern for us for the early years. And we greatly enjoyed it, Jonathan and I, with little David an attentive adherent across the table, learning to write upside down!

But it was difficult to preserve school time intact

from interruption, nor could the Miri environment supply the broad educational spectrum we desired for our sons. Chefoo School could. Deeply grateful to God for Chefoo, its caring and capable staff, its rich hundred year tradition, we planned and prepared Jonathan and David to enter boarding school at the end of our next furlough, when they would be seven and eight.

Furlough was a real strain, lived in the awareness of this coming major break of the tight family bonds. Because of the inevitable insecurity for two young children in our movable environment, we had chosen to make ourselves personally the central pole of their security structure. Now we faced losing at one stroke our two precious and protected sons. To ignore the impending separation was impossible, with two hundred nametags to sew on. Our marriage would have to be reshaped to suit eight months a year on our own, and for the second time a radical change of lifestyle loomed for me since the boys had largely constituted my raison d'être for eight years. Being well acquainted with the Lord's ways I knew I would cope but I could not see *how* I would cope. I was face to face with the empty nest syndrome[1] early and in an acute form. Meanwhile we had the actual parting to get through.

"That's my sad hanky, Mum." Jonathan reclaimed the sturdy paper handkerchief I was about to throw out of his pockets at our nightstop in the

[1] The empty nest syndrome refers to the crisis of confidence and self-worth and the major change of role a mother faces when her last child leaves home.

Kuala Lumpur mission home on our way to Chefoo. He had been given it in the Singapore airport to mop up his dripping tears as we left Dad behind. He needed it for only an initial night's weeping as a new boy in the big dorm. I bought a boxful for myself.

There is no better distraction, when one is tied in all but visible knots, to handling four children new to boarding school — one unpredictable, one showing off, one composed (thank goodness) and one who was carsick before we even left Kuala Lumpur. Once the children had moved into the school they were highly excited and happy as larry, and I was left to take my superfluous person back to the holiday bungalow a mile away and start in on the box of tissues. What tremendously understanding and empathetic fellow-guests I had. No one minded prolonged absences or took undue notice of red eyes. A loving, understanding shoulder was always available. Someone even slipped the dog's chain so it did not howl under my window for a second interminable night.

Sunday still had to be got through, with an unbelievably inappropriate sermon adjuring us to sacrifice all for the Lord's sake. My world did not have anything left worth sacrificing! Eventually the day wore on to bedtime, and I kissed one toothpastey lad and last glimpsed the other sitting diffidently on his patchwork quilt showing his treasured new computer game to a couple of old hands — who dismissed it as juvenile. A sharp little etching on the mind.

Letters from homeside wellwishers were not always understanding. One or two were intolerably hurtful. Missionary mothers facing the empty nest syndrome do not appreciate facile sermons from folks who know little of its acutely sensitive reality. Such folk can be a support if they are able to convey, "I don't presume to know what you're going through but I love you and your kids and I'm there with you in caring prayer." Nor is being praised for one's self-sacrificing obedience particularly helpful, since it lays one open to pride and self-pity. Those who have walked the selfsame path of pain-filled self-denial can indeed help with their understanding words and advice, drawn from their own crucible experience. Even communicating one's love to children from hundreds of miles away proved an art to be learned.

Thus down the hill in Kuala Lumpur I began painfully to rebuild my shattered world and refill my emptied nest, with what was planned to be a six weeks' Malay language refresher course and turned out to be part-time running the mission home. We had realized I would need an absorbing job and companionship at this time when Brian had to be in Singapore for a month's meetings, and these the mission home situation supplied. There were compatriots to laugh with, new colleagues to build a relationship with, older missionaries for counsel, and members of other missions to share enriching experiences. How marvellously sensitive the Lord's attention to detail is.

Fortunately I had been long enough in OMF to

know that a worthwhile job invariably materializes, and during our years in Indonesia, Singapore and Malaysia I had experienced an interesting variety of them.

But ... women's work? I was positively surprised to find myself becoming interested in a job done, I had subconsciously presumed, by those incapable of anything more worthy! A group of us had begun a women's Bible study and seen it grow from nine to ninety. Miri is full of oilmen and civil servants and it seemed most husbands worked offshore on the rigs or travelled upriver. My husband also spent forty percent of his time away from home, so we could identify together in the demands of alternately taking full responsibility for home and extended family, and slipping back into the adapting role when the head of the house returned. I had, however, an advantage most of my friends did not have, a sensitive and practising Christian husband. Together we discovered what a tremendous mutual support women could be to one another and saw the Lord change first ourselves, then friends, circumstances, children and even some husbands.

Thus I became genuinely interested in women's work and, suspecting this was to be my major task for the next term of service, began not very enthusiastically to rebuild my caved-in roof on it — only to discover that interest alone was not a sufficiently sturdy structure for a new roof. Interest needed to be supported by the beams of a willing, committed, dependent spirit.

Willingness was foundational on the Lord's list. I

had never been a good sleeper. When the boys came I probably still got a punctuated version of my five hours a night but the strain was greater and the rewards less, and I became dependent on tranquillisers at night and coffee during the day. Eventually I felt I should try at least switching to decaffeinated coffee, only to discover I had inadvertently been drinking it for three weeks without perceiving the difference! But I was afraid to relinquish the security of a pill-ensured sleep not, strangely enough, because I felt I could not cope without sleep, but because the sleeping business seemed like a gate which, if I let the Lord open it, would lead me down paths outside my regulated world. Graciously the Lord refused to allow me to dodge that gate, bringing me one night to such impatience with my puerile prevarications that I was prepared to get decisive about obeying Him and put away my pills. This involved practical effort like setting a lights-out time, reading inconsequential books, and refusing to go back on the decision when I happened not to sleep well or faced an important task the next day. It worked! I could barely believe it. The wonder of that liberation to normalcy has never left me.

Commitment to specific action was the second beam for my roof, and with this I was squarely caught from backing down on my willingness. I attended the Sabah and Sarawak Women's Fellowship conference representing some fifteen thousand women of the Evangelical Church of Borneo, where the "in thing" was to demand a week's course on leadership in your district during the coming year.

God used the president, a delightful lady of no finesse, to put me right on the spot demanding, "Will you conduct these leadership courses?" You can't say a convincing no to fifty eager faces so I opted for yes — and was nailed down to start in March.

I felt I was attending my own execution when I set off for that first course, willing, committed, prepared and dead scared. There isn't by nature an ounce of adventure in my make-up. Added to that, I had been seventeen years married and had seldom travelled or worked alone since my single teacher days. The old Fokker Friendship flew out of Miri at dusk for Kota Kinabalu as I concentratedly wrote postcards to ignore my tension. In the rainy twilight a perfect, vivid rainbow encircled the plane with an undeniable totality.

God gentled me into the job. He never required me to adapt to everything immediately. There was a drought on in Sabah those months, which meant bathing in the river half a mile away. I was no expert at the two-*sarong*-one-towel-wriggle routine for bathing in the river, nor had I ever shared a room with local folk. I didn't have to. A sensitive older missionary lady invited me to use her bathroom; the other women were too shy at that stage to share my room; and under duress my fluency in Malay returned with a rush and a dictionary.

Over the next six months my urbanized self learnt how to manage rural living, one task at a time. To sleep on the floor, all turn together; to change discreetly in public under a *sarong*; to cope with bedbugs and toilets without doors; to be continually surrounded by yet another unfamiliar tribal language; to produce sermons, advice, gracious speeches in Malay without warning; and to understand what distressed souls were saying and what they actually meant.

Gradually the Lord re-erected my roof over a wider-opened house. It was difficult to reshape our marriage with its constant changes from parent to Darby and Joan to grass widowhood. I had to learn to manage on my own when Brian was travelling. It has never become easy to part with our boys or to share with local women how much personal pain was involved in the blessing all of us participate in during a week's teaching course. My voice usually wobbled and the women sniffed and sleeved away their tears. But I came to New Year's Day feeling unafraid for the first time I can remember, because I had learnt by vivid experience how infinitely able the Lord is to handle all circumstances faced in His name, because He had given and taught me more of himself in one year than I had been ready to learn for twenty.

The joy of a worthwhile job well done; genuine close friendship and an amazing amount of fun with fellow teachers; loosening of tightly held fears; perception of the vast opportunities and needs among women; tremendous scope for teaching and counselling on issues that were just as current and real for me too; and the chance to do it all again the following year on marriage and family life. It adds up to a healthy credit balance.

Kesanggupan in Malay indicates willingness, sense of responsibility, capacity. "Our *kesanggupan* (which) is the work of the Lord"[2] makes a very strong structure for a new extended roof, and I don't regret the old one in spite of the wounds and bruises its cave-in dealt me.

[2]   2 Cor. 3:5 from the Indonesian Bible.

Ian & Lyn McNickle, *from New Zealand, work among the tribal people of Taiwan.*

When I Am Weak ...

The day began with an air of excitement as we all helped to pack a picnic lunch and get the last minute things together for our much-looked-forward-to holiday, over the mountains to Hualien on the east coast of Taiwan. Our three children had been away at Chefoo School in Malaysia, and already several weeks of their time at home had slipped by quickly. Christmas, filled with the excitement of just being together, receiving many cards reminding us of loved ones in the homeland, singing carols by candlelight, and the many other things that go to make Christmas a special time, had all come and gone. Now it was time for a holiday and rest from the busyness of life.

As the boys got the last of their treasures together and ten-year-old Lisa filled the flask with hot water, in walked Gisela and Margaret, our two newest workers to the field. We were their senior missionaries and so they came to bid us farewell.

"We want to share a very special custom with

you which we have in Switzerland," said Margaret. "On New Year's Eve, we share promises from God's Word together. But as you won't be here then I have brought along several promises, and want you to pick one to take with you into the new year." Carefully I selected one card which read ....

"For He has charged his angels to guard you wherever you go." (Psalm 91:11).

"How appropriate," I thought as I thanked Margaret and Gisela; but little did I realize how meaningful and significant those words would be later in the day.

By lunchtime we were high in the mountains, and stopped to enjoy our picnic lunch beside a quiet flowing stream. The air was crisp and fresh, and not too far away we could see the snow-capped hills displayed in all their brilliance with a clear blue sky in the background. It was so quiet and relaxing, and our hearts warmed towards God as we considered the beauty of His creation. How good it was to be alive and a part of God's great world! At two p.m. we were on our way again, climbing ever so slowly in our station wagon over the steep hills to nine thousand feet above sea level. As we rounded one corner and were about to curve into the next bend, we caught sight of another car travelling too fast and unable to take the corner.

CRASH!!

In an instant everything came to a standstill.

With shaking legs and a prayer in our hearts, we were able to climb out. Together we surveyed the damage, and the young driver of the other car promptly sent his passenger off in a passing car to call the police. Our family joined hands in a circle on the side of the road to thank God that we were alive and unharmed, and to ask His help in this lonely and desolate place.

Several hours passed before a heavy truck arrived on the scene. It was carting scrap metal from Hualien to Changhua on the west coast, and had been hired by the young man responsible for the accident. Eventually we managed to get his car up on top of the scrap metal, and ours was hooked up behind to be towed back down to Taichung. The children and I climbed into the cab of this huge truck, feeling a sense of importance from sitting up there high above all the other traffic! We were tired, hungry and suffering from shock, but thankful that at least we were heading home again.

Sitting in a prominent place in the cab was a small idol with incense sticks burning. "It's supposed to help give us a safe journey," the driver told me as I began to witness to him about our unseen God who could see us wherever we are and who had truly protected us that day. Below the idol shelf was the usual stereo tape deck with loud pop music blaring out as if to keep the idol awake! With three upset children and feeling rather shaken up myself, I felt I would crack if I had to keep listening to this loud music. So I asked if I could put on some of the children's cassettes. What a comfort and relief it was to listen to "Kids' Praise" — albeit coming from below the idol shelf!

It was a long slow journey down the mountain, and we did not reach Taichung till almost midnight. Then we discovered that most of our luggage had fallen out of the back of the car on the way! Still, we enjoyed the hot drink and the comfort of our own beds, and how we thanked God that indeed His protecting angels had been around us.

The next morning the news spread quickly to our fellow workers, whose love and concern both then and over the next weeks were a great source of strength and encouragement to us. One friend took Ian on his motorbike to see if they could recover any luggage, but their efforts were all in vain. Not only did we all lose clothes, but gone forever was my precious Bible, and my large stamp collection. It was to have been a holiday project to put them all into the new album my husband had just given me for Christmas. Insurance and repairs took a while to sort out. And worst of all, Ian suffered a slipped disc as a result of the accident and was confined to bed. I was able to nurse him at home, but he was in traction, and several weeks slipped by with no improvement. In fact he got worse and worse, requiring high doses of sedative and pain relief.

The jump from being an extremely active person to suddenly being confined to bed with excruciating pain was hard for Ian to take. As he lay there helpless for two weeks, then three, then four and more, the days seemed long and dreary, full of depression, and many were the sleepless nights. Nothing seemed to hold any meaning as Ian wondered if our whole missionary career was in jeopardy.

Blessings out of Buffeting, by Alan Redpath lay beside his bed, and as Ian read this he thought through again the letters Paul wrote to the Corinthian Church. At one of his very low points he was forcibly reminded of the verse, "... when I am weak, then I am strong ..." (2 Cor. 12:10). Paul was talking about taking pleasure in infirmities and distresses! This was a new perspective, something to hang on to in the dark. God was reminding us both that He was there, that even in extreme weakness one could be strong in Him. As Ian lay thinking through our past term of service, it all seemed like nothing. God helped him to see that we do so much in our own strength, perhaps just to prove our effectiveness. But only what is done in God and in His way will be of lasting value. We began to realize afresh that it is our personal relationship to God which is of far more importance than all the work we do for Him, and it is here that our strength lies.

Chinese New Year went by and now it was time for the three children to return to Chefoo School. There was the usual bustle of last minute packing, but gone was the usual excitement as the children had to leave their Dad in such pain. A fellow missionary had come to look after Ian while I took the children to the airport.

As usual, before we left home we committed each other and our travels to the Lord, praying for His protection and over-ruling in the affairs of the day.

Chinese New Year is holiday time when hundreds of people travel, and this day was no exception. We had reserved seats on the bus from Taichung to Taoyuan, where another missionary family would meet us and take us on to the airport. Our bus was overcrowded in typical Asian style, but we were thankful at least to have our seats in the front of the bus, and as it pulled out of the bus station I sat back and relaxed.

The bus pulled to a stop at the traffic lights and in that instant I was jolted out of my relaxation. I had no passports for the children! Plane tickets are always held by the OMF office in Taipei, and normally it is Ian's concern to make sure passports and so on are in order, while my job is the packing. This time Ian was in such agony that the thought of passports had not even crossed his mind, and with so much else to think of I had completely forgotten them too! But God intervened. We had committed the day to Him, and in His own unique way He reminded me before we reached the point of no return.

I bolted out of my seat to tell the driver my dilemma. "You had better get off, go home and get another bus," he told me calmly. However, I knew that that was impossible. If we all got off this bus there would be no way we could make it to the airport on time.

But in those few split seconds before the lights turned green, the Lord gave me an idea.

"I'll leave the children on the bus," I told the driver, "and if you will let me off, I'll get a taxi home and meet the bus before you go on the Super Highway."

"Okay," said the driver and opened the bus door. Quickly I told the children not to worry, "just stay right here and I'll soon be back." Fortunately our home was in the northern section of town, and while the bus worked its way across town I sped home in a taxi, rushed inside, found the passports while explaining to Ian what had happened, and dived back into the taxi which sped the last few kilometers out to the Super Highway. The bus had pulled up just a few minutes ahead of us. Out I hopped and, with shaking legs and a very thankful heart, climbed back into the waiting bus.

What a warm welcome I got from all the passengers, not least my three children! In my haste I had omitted to tell them at what point I would rejoin the bus, and I was sure that as they approached the Highway, their fears that I would not return in time would be mounting. During my taxi ride I had prayed the Lord would keep them calm, and so He had. As I offered them my profuse apologies, they replied quite brightly, "Don't worry, Mum, everyone looked after us — see — they gave us grapes and oranges ..." I quickly ate some sweets to help restore calm to my shaking body and then we as a family, there and then on the crowded bus, thanked God for his over-ruling. How good is the God we adore!

It was when the moment came for final farewells at the airport that I most missed the support of my husband, for although the children went off happily the heart strings are still pulled tight when they finally disappear through that formidable immigration door! It was a quiet and sad journey back to Taichung. How desolate I felt — my three children all gone and my husband lying on his back in agony, unable to move without excruciating pain. "Lord, what's it all for?" my thoughts questioned. "Why do we go through these agonies — what does the future hold anyway ....?" I had few answers, but I was assured of the very presence of God in the midst of the troubles.

By the time I arrived home at seven p.m. I was exhausted, for a lot had happened since I left eleven hours before. I had barely finished eating supper when in walked our missionary doctor friend who had Ian under his care. After prescribing even stronger drugs he finally said to us, "I think the best thing for you to do is to get home to New Zealand as quickly as possible, any way you can, and have surgery. Ian's condition is deteriorating and traction is doing no good ...."

"What do we do now ...?" I cried out to God. Having had experience of sending stretcher cases by plane, we knew it required four first class seats. "Lord, it will cost us the earth, just to get home, and even then surgery for this kind of thing is not always successful ... Lord, what should we do ...?"

Our hearts were heavy that night. The children had gone and the future seemed bleak. But over the next few days the Lord slowly restored His peace to our troubled hearts. Three different people called up and suggested we visit a local Chinese doctor, all independently recommending a Christian who was elder of the big Baptist church in town and who was trained in both Western medicine and acupuncture. After three acupuncture treatments, Ian was once again able to take our dog for a walk to the nearby rice fields. That was a miracle! It still took several weeks of treatment before we were able to leave for furlough, but praise God, as strength returned and healing came we were able to consider the trip home.

Again we could see how God had intervened. In our distress we had called out to Him and He had heard our voices. As we looked back over the two and a half months from the time of our accident until we left for furlough, we could only thank God that through it all He was there, and that when we needed Him most, He led us on and provided a way for us. To God be the glory.

Mary Bates *has worked in the Philippines for nearly twenty years.*

We Sat Where They Sat

My co-worker Elvi had gone to Manila on her way to furlough, and I was clearing up after a pastors' conference in our house — we'd had five adults and three toddlers sleeping in my room, and nine pastors in the other rooms! During that morning I talked to various friends from church, and then settled down to prepare a Bible Study on James 1:1-12, where verse 2 says: "Count it all joy, my brethren, when you encounter various trials ...". I never did get round to giving this study, except to myself!

It was very hot, and a power cut meant no electricity to work the fans. So in the early afternoon I decided to have a siesta, and to work late at night when it would be cooler. I was tired, so went straight to sleep and didn't hear the doorbell, nor the church bells clanging madly. Finally I awoke to the sound of rushing feet and cries of "Fire, fire!" I went outside to investigate, and found the fire was in the street at the back of our house!

With real God-given peace in my heart I returned indoors, collected my typewriter, tape recorder, passport and a few clothes, and took them to a church member's home, two streets away. When I got back the house behind, only three to four feet from ours, was now blazing. What should I rescue next? The training materials we had prepared? Elvi's organ or Honda? As I went up the stairs eight to ten young people suddenly arrived, sent by the policeman friend who had rung the bell and, getting no reply, thought I was out. They staggered out with three of Elvi's trunks and the fridge, which disgorged its contents on the stairs and wasted ten precious minutes. They also took out our stove, calor gas tanks, wireless and spirit duplicator, but these got lost in the chaos. They were thoughtful enough to empty my underwear drawer into a blanket and throw it over the balcony! We saved most of the training materials, but all our books, files, lessons and teaching aids were no more. Some could be easily replaced but others represented hours, even months, of hard work. The cat also perished.

When we left, the fire was into our kitchen. I didn't actually *see* the house burn right down, because I was trying to locate Elvi's Honda. By 7 p.m. half the town centre was burnt to the ground, and our belongings were scattered all over the town. A friend had phoned Elvi in Manila, and she and one of the church leaders came straight back down to Gumaca, finally locating me just after midnight. I was so happy to see them and glad to show Elvi her saved organ, only to realise that her much-more-expensive accordion had perished in the flames.

Friends from another mission had also made a special trip to Batangas to tell our OMF superintendent, whose phone was out of order. He and his wife got the news at midnight, and left at 5 a.m. to come to us. That was Sunday. We were able to go to church, to have lunch with the believers and locate most of our bits and pieces, and then go to Manila in the superintendent's pick-up in the evening. We were very, very tired, but still had that inner peace and joy from the Lord.

This was our fourth fire in Gumaca in the fifteen months we had lived there, and by far the worst. The other big one was in the market a year before, and I was shaking after that even though it didn't hit us. So the peace I experienced when our own house was destroyed was a special gift from above!

The damage was devastating. Half the commercial centre was destroyed, and well over three thousand of the population of nine thousand was homeless. The blaze raged for six hours. Strong winds from the sea, the hot season, lack of water and an inefficient fire brigade all added to the speedy devastation. Many spent the night in the Town Hall or railway station. Wonderfully, no one was killed or seriously injured, and no other church members were affected except the Chinese businessman on whose premises it all started. Did fat in the frying pan catch fire? Or did someone ignite his warehouse? Many rumours as to the cause were flying around.

We were so well taken care of, with good food, a home to sleep in, and the loving, prayerful concern of the church members. It was an experience we would not have missed, though we have no desire to go through it again! Soon it began to prove a real help in local relationships. Ezekiel "sat where they sat"; well, we burnt where they burnt!

The Burden
Is
Lightness

We were sitting at the kitchen table, that evening before Valentine's Day 1983, chatting with our superintendent who occasionally stopped by to see how things were going. Sensitively he introduced the subject of our teenage daughter thousands of miles away at boarding school, and that was when my heart seemed to leap into my throat.

There had been a problem of weight loss between July and November. Letters from Ellen's dorm parents had revealed how they'd become alarmed at her thinness, and after observing that she was eating less and less had suspected anorexia nervosa. They had her in the hospital for extensive tests which showed there were no physical malfunctions. Then they began a campaign to get her to eat, with the help of the school psychologist. We had been shocked and worried, but somewhat reassured by letters saying that they had caught it early, they were giving their utmost, and Ellen was responding positively. Of course we were praying constantly for the situation, as were our fellow-workers and national Christian friends. But occasionally, even though our basic attitude was one of trust in the Lord, I still had visions of her dying of malnutrition in some unforeseen turn for the worse.

Then she had come home for Christmas vacation and we'd been relieved that, although she was still too thin, at least she was not skeletal or haggard. She was eating fairly well, and we were praising God that through the care and efforts of the dorm parents and school counselor, and through the Lord's help, she had come out of the woods. We had had many anxious moments during that vacation though, because we had been told that if she wasn't up to one hundred pounds by the end of three weeks, she couldn't go back to school with the group. Would she make the grade? It seemed very unlikely. What would we do with her then? The Lord would work it out for the best, we concluded — we'd just have to trust Him. In the end, Ellen and her sister got a special one-week extension of vacation, plus a last-minute permission from the medical advisor to go back even though she was several pounds below standard.

Now, a month later, our superintendent was gently telling us that Ellen was not keeping her weight up as well as they'd hoped, and not being too cooperative in eating. The dorm parents were understandably worried and frustrated. Mission leaders in conference with medical personnel had decided that if she didn't improve dramatically she would need hospitalization, and we would have to leave the field immediately and rush her home. So we should be prepared at any time to receive an emergency phone call telling us to pack up and go.

When I heard this I felt as if a sword was suspended by a thread above our heads. We pictured Ellen emaciated and needing hospitalization; we thought of what it would mean to drop all the work we had been doing and leave others to pick up the pieces. I spent a sleepless night wondering what had happened to previous answers to prayer — was God's help only a temporary thing? Was more prayer the answer? Anyway we posed ourselves to wait for the possible fatal phone call.

The very next day, mercifully, one of the faster letters arrived from the dorm parents (in five days instead of ten). It reported progress and encouragement, with Ellen's weight on the up-turn. Now we felt as if the sword was suspended by a cord rather than a thread, but still we had to be ready for anything. Meanwhile the Lord was always giving us the ability to put our burden in a separate compartment away from the work that we were doing for him — the needs of the people we were ministering to, the daily pressing duties. I would often skip lunch on Wednesday and use the time praying that Ellen would have a healthier attitude toward food. Letters became even more positive and we knew the phone call wouldn't come. The dorm parents were loving and patient; the school counselor was having regular sessions with Ellen; she was almost up to a hundred pounds.

That May we were due for furlough as soon as

our daughters finished school. We felt it was well-timed. Ellen would be home with us, and would probably gain more weight and get over this anorexia tendency entirely. Our travel reading for the plane trip included a book on anorexia, *The Golden Cage*. We felt pretty well-informed by now through various articles people had sent us to read. But we still couldn't figure out the psychological mechanism behind the problem in Ellen's case. Even experts made the causes sound rather uncertain — it could have something to do with a perfectionist mother, a fear of growing up, anger turned inward, and a need to feel in control of one aspect of one's life — this all bound up with modern Western society's fetish of slimness.

In Ellen's case there was a suggestion that it might have to do with feelings of being abandoned. She remembered one occasion when her father had been an escort on the train to boarding school, and had stayed around for a few days before making the trip back. That night she had cried and felt as if she had been abandoned. Actually, most missionary children experience this feeling at one time or another, but it is usually temporary, and they don't doubt their parents love for them. Ellen had spent seven basically happy years at boarding school, with three months home for vacations every year. We didn't believe the Lord would lead us into a situation that would cause emotional deprivation and damage to our daughter.

During our furlough Ellen had regular sessions with a professional Christian counselor for nine months, which gave her an opportunity to express past and present feelings. Toward the end the counselor made quite a positive assessment of her emotional health. When the time came to think about returning to the field, we had to be open to the possibility that Ellen would prefer to remain with her parents at this stage rather than returning to boarding school. But whenever the possibility of staying in the USA came up she was adamant about wanting to return "home" to Southeast Asia.

We are still puzzled about our daughter. At the end of a year's furlough she has not gained an ounce above what she was at the beginning. But we believe the Lord's way for us is to return to the field. We believe His ways with us are perfect. We believe that He often works slowly, always thoroughly, and that "whatever God does endures forever."

Margaret Kirk *is now back in Indonesia, teaching theology in a remote corner of the island of Sulawesi.*

He Makes My Way Perfect

I eagerly opened the envelope that had been delivered, its foreign stamps already delicately removed by some enthusiast in the postal service. Inside was an informal photo of guests at a party. There was my petite, gray-haired mother almost lost in the great armchair but looking utterly joyous, as well she might on the occasion of her eldest granddaughter's wedding. Sitting on the arm of the chair was my long-legged father, smiling too — but there was something wrong! He looked gaunt, almost haunted, with his features sharpened by weight loss and tell-tale dark circles under his eyes. Or was it just that I hadn't seen him for three years and the aging process was taking its toll?

Father was a plain man; to us, his family, he was the essence of stability, the epitome of integrity, the kind of person that one thinks of as going on forever. He looked after mother who had become too frail and forgetful to run their home. He also tended his exquisitely manicured garden where all growing things thrived because he talked lovingly to them. When there was time he enjoyed the company of his peers in various retirement activities.

His cheerful letter followed the photo — having surgery, a friend will stay with mother for the period of hospitalization, and not to worry.

Then my brother's telegram came. Everything had gone wrong, malignancy (I might have guessed), complications following difficult surgery, extended aftercare. They had taken mother to be with them in the city some two hundred miles away where another brother also lived.

"Please come home for a while at least," they begged.

The telegram had been received by OMF in Jakarta three weeks previously! Inter-island communications in those days left much to be desired, particularly when trying to communicate with someone in Central Sulawesi. Perhaps my father was dead by now? A thoughtful superintendent had added his footnote to the long telegram — "All praying here — will back your decision."

My location in the province of Central Sulawesi had been something of a redeployment move and is a story in itself: sufficient to say that, despite the "isolation", I loved it. I loved the people, my Indonesian colleagues, the opportunity and the freedom to work out one's own strategy in a many-faceted Bible teaching ministry with a needy church. And I had plans for next furlough. Back at my alma mater I would complete a master's degree in Christian Education — perhaps a doctorate.

Everyone was doing it, or seemed to be, and nothing could be more acceptable in the long-term strategy of helping build the church in Indonesia.

Now came the agony of leaving something full of potential, something unfinished — for leave I must! Even if the news that father was dead and buried was following, there was mother. It was then that I truly appreciated the attitude of Asians towards family.

"Why, you will go home, of course," said they. No alternative entered their heads.

My colleagues divided up my teaching responsibilities amongst themselves and, in three days, household effects were either packed or distributed.

Travel in Central Sulawesi was in no way connected with timetables. When there were enough passengers a vehicle departed, if there was a vehicle. That was all. But my only foreign colleagues in the province at that time, a jovial Dutchman and his family from the Protestant Church in Holland, had a vehicle! He wound his four-wheel-drive around the mountain road to Poso, our port, with the abandon of a modern Jehu. That same night there was a little boat that dodged among the coral reefs as it chugged along the coast to Parigi with myself and ten others. There another vehicle, actually looking for passengers, carried us over another hair-raising mountain road to Palu.

Meanwhile, back in Poso, my Dutch friend was working persuasively with the police to get a radio message to Palu and a seat for me on the plane to Jakarta. With two hours to spare I was on that plane, so a journey that could have taken as long as the telegram proved miraculously uncomplicated.

For a whole day superintendent George Steed weaved among Jakarta's traffic from office to office, deftly cutting through a swathe of red tape as only he was able. By midnight I was again airborn, and the afternoon of the next day was in New Zealand. It was Easter. The Lord had indeed "gone before."

My brother's boisterous young family of five was all lined up at the airport for a welcome. I almost passed by a little old lady, rather bedraggled, standing uncertainly as if not part of the group; only her eyes beseeching to be recognized. It was mother! The shock and sudden transplantation had left their mark in lostness and bewilderment.

The next day mother and I flew home. Father had been discharged from hospital to his elderly sister's little flat. He had had a coronary while convalescing and was a stooped and weary old man.

Being back together in their own home worked magic. Just having someone there lifting the responsibility of running the place from Dad, brought back his spirit and appetite. Quite quickly he was out and about, walking in the garden, pulling up weeds, watching the birds. Mother, spruced but frail, alternated between her serene and gracious self and the mental confusion of which she was painfully aware. I studied and endeavoured to practice the cooking arts from her cookbooks, which pleased her no end, and cared fondly for father's garden under his minute directions till he grew in strength and was doing it for himself. The seasons passed. The garden received its winter pruning, and one day my father said rather flatly:

"I suppose you will be wanting to get back. We will miss you, but we'll manage somehow with the home help service. We can have 'meals on wheels' delivered if I get tired of cooking."

Was that what I had been waiting to hear? I thought it was. Hormone control of father's type of malignancy was highly effective long term, the doctor said. I commenced negotiations to return.

Then father collapsed in his garden — another heart attack!

Somehow I hadn't got the right message, and it was clear I needed to reappraise God's purpose for our family at this time. I stood at father's bedside in the coronary care unit reading the question in his eyes — the question he would never ask.

"I'll not go back as long as you need me ...."

The anxiety faded and he slept. I eyed the jumpy, uneven red line that was being traced by the heart monitor above the bed.

I shall always be grateful for Michael Griffiths' words: "Christ speaks severely to those who neglect the clear command of God about responsibility to support one's parents on the alleged grounds that they have higher spiritual responsibilities ... When parents are old and weak and needing care which no one else can give, the missionary is normally bound to return home to fulfil his or her responsibilities, and to do it joyfully and cheerfully without any sense of frustration or conflict of loyalties."[1]

My parents cherished their home, their independence and the dignity it bestowed. They could only continue to keep it if someone lived with them. A move to an institution was unthinkable. They would have had to leave the town and their friends. The elderly do not transplant easily and some not at all.

So I formally withdrew from the mission and started to look for a job. It is then that it hits you, that term "professional suicide." Originally I had qualified as a nurse and been involved in medical ministry in Indonesia, until a government decision that foreign medical personnel would no longer be given permits to work led to redeployment. All my former nursing colleagues still in the job were at the top. I would have done anything but there was nothing, neither in my profession nor in any other sphere in the small town where my parents had always lived. I had held charge positions, worked and studied in a country other than my own before ever learning a foreign language in order to teach in an Indonesian hospital. It was humiliating!

At last came the opportunity for a relieving position with the Health Department, but it was in the next town, sixty miles away. They offered some orientation and I took the job. During the work week I hired morning househelp for my parents. In

[1] *Give up Your Small Ambitions*, page 100.

the afternoons friends came, some of Dad's old cronies or ladies from the church. How grateful I was for their kindness they probably never realized. The deal was viable financially and my parents were happier when I was working. Weekends were for them.

It was winter, and part of the daily journey was over an icy mountain road. I prayed as I drove that the car would not slip into the gorge or another vehicle slide into it, and that no emergency situation would arise at home while I was not there.

So the months slipped by, highlighted with visits from the families in the city. I saw both old people deteriorating. Father's malignancy was not being controlled by the hormone therapy and its secondary manifestations in spine and thigh bones gradually decreased his mobility. Deafness bothered him — the degenerative deafness of old age that no hearing aid can really help. Mother's frailty prevented her from raising her voice so that he could hear. By then too, her sentences frequently stopped unfinished because she had forgotten how she began them. When she wrote to the families in the city it took all day, and I would be asked to check and reconstruct her faltering thoughts so that her correspondence might be understood.

My father often grumbled about his "useless hulk" and had a fierce dread of becoming bed-ridden. During his last months this drove him to a daily struggle to get to the couch in the living room, where at least he could look at mother reclining on the other couch and see garden and birds through the window.

There he who scarcely ever read more than the newspaper was deeply impressed by *The General next to God*, the biography of William Booth of the Salvation Army. He who had little taste for music other than a birdsong, listened to George Beverly Shea singing "He's got the whole wide world in His hands" and observed: "That Shea fellow — let's hear him again. I can understand every word he is saying. None of the tum-te-tum beat stuff to mess it up." A reticent sort of Christian, he knew he was dying and that we also knew; but one did not talk about such things.

Medically speaking, the bedridden state was inevitable. I dreaded it too, and began to make arrangements with the hospital visiting nurse to set aside for us the various pieces of equipment that would be needed. She was also a friend and a member of our church, a Scottish woman who had nursed her husband through terminal illness.

"Don't worry, lass," she consoled. "We don't know how these things will happen, but when the time comes, God will give you the strength." Our doctor was kindness itself, and I was full of admiration for modern drug therapy to keep pain controlled and life bearable. "You matter to the last moment of your life," assures Dr Cecily Saunders, famous for her care of the dying, "and we will do all we can to help you, not only to die peacefully but to live until you die." Those words became part of my experience.

On the last day of his life the struggle from bed to couch was terrifying, but my father had to do it. One of my brothers phoned to say they were coming at the weekend and bringing a grandchild. That raised a smile. In the afternoon a most faithful friend called and offered to shave him — something he had never let me do. They joked a little. That evening, extreme weakness. He lay with eyes closed. His arm slipped off the edge of the couch and hung there limply. I grasped the hand, lifting the arm back by his side and feeling an answering grip! Without opening his eyes he smiled, then settled himself lower to sleep. I held the pale, almost transparent hand till his breathing became regular, then noisy.

After mother was settled for the night, I went back to the sitting room and lay down on her day couch. All night stertorous breathing filled the room. "He's not asleep — he's in a coma," I thought.

The change in breathing must have wakened me out of my doze before dawn. It was unmistakable — the familiar crescendo, subsiding to almost nothing, then increasing again. I sprang up. My father was dying. Again I took the transparent hand and found myself stroking his forehead and praying "Lord, receive his spirit ...." until his breathing faded for the last time. He lay there as if taking his usual nap, his white hair glistening in the lamplight. Dignified and independent to the last, he had not even died in his bed! I knew then what that last hand squeeze and smile had meant.

"Thank you Lord, for taking him in such a kindly

way," I whispered, and went to wake mother. She was so calm, I wondered at first if she had understood, but I think she was glad for him. Then she, who could rarely complete a sentence without forgetting how she began, said:

"Well, come and get some rest now. You can phone doctor and the boys when it's light."

The funeral was a blur. I had taken holiday leave to be at home during the last part of father's illness, but now would have to give up that job to be with mother. Once again loomed the problem of finding work of any sort for a middle-aged citizen who had spent more of her life out of the country than in it. I sent in my resignation. Then a marvellous thing happened — the Health Department offered to arrange an exchange transfer. My new office would be within walking distance and I could be home with mother for lunch each day. I could even pop in on my rounds as town Public Health nurse!

We had six good months together, during which time she was persuaded to do many things that in her frailty she had not attempted for a long time. A cheery househelp came mornings, and friends from the church fellowship kept an afternoon call roster during my work week. They did almost all the talking and mother just listened. It suited her well.

Then an ambulance took her off, following a night heart seizure.

"She would be better in the hospital," said the doctor. "She's likely to have another one. Her arteries are shot!" I knew that was true, but she rallied, and I went to see about the feasibility of taking her home. The doctor met me in the corridor.

"Your mother's just had a massive stroke," he said.

She could still smile recognition, but was unable to communicate. A few more days and she slipped into unconsciousness and died also.

When two people who have spent fifty years together are not parted for long, there is a fittingness. But for me, I had twice witnessed the end of a lifetime and felt it to be my own.

Another funeral. My brothers and families and relatives departed. Our dear old aunt, father's sister, spent a couple of nights with me and then there was just myself in the empty house, haunted with memories. But it was a good haunting. These had been special, different years, that could not help but add to me and bring a fuller appreciation of the values inherited from these two who had passed through death's mysterious gateway to a new dimension of life.

> "One cares for a little child for what he
>   will become.
> One cares for the aged for what they
>   have been."

Again, I could only say thank you to God that He saw I was there when they both so needed someone, to make the contribution that no one else was in a position to make — the unique, distinctive ministry of the single daughter. It is often so.

I had left home as a permanent resident at the age of eighteen, and travelled extensively before ever I heard the Lord speak to me about missionary service. Yet the home contact remained. Home was always there with its stability "like the bow that shoots the arrow." Mother had been the correspondent until she realised she was no longer capable, and she had kept every letter that I had written. This amazing fact I discovered when cleaning out cupboards at her instructions.

"You can have them now. If the day comes when you have time on your hands you can ... you can ...." She had forgotten. Her voice trailed off in frustration.

"You mean write a book!" I supplied, laughing at the thought.

"Yes, something like that ...." It was then that I started drafting a plan partly to please her.

Afterwards, filling in the empty months my mother knew would come, I finished the book. And I had clung to that job as small-town district nurse. Based in the old home and surrounded by father's beautiful garden, I majored in family health needs; visiting, listening, counselling, struggling on behalf of those who for a variety of reasons were not making the grade as functioning families, and for the little-known underprivileged of our affluent society, the deprived children "born to fail". There was plenty to do, but the thought kept niggling in the back of my mind that there were plenty of people to do it too.

Mother's faith had perspective and realism. She had been known to say to her friends: "When I have gone to Heaven, then Margaret will be back to Indonesia." I knew it was her hope that I return.

What about the studies in Christian Education —

the doctorate? I had already been five years at home. It was too late. A younger person would have to do that. I confess, I still felt disappointment, but it did not really matter. God had ministered to my grief by keeping me busy.

I made plans to return. The visa came through easily, and that year the book[2] was published. Through my wise and discerning mother a dormant gift had been brought to life and with it, new possibilities for service.

In retrospect what can I say? Just this: "Thank you Lord that it happened like that."

"... God's ways are perfect ... He makes my way perfect."

El Shaddai, the all sufficient One, had watched over my stumbling efforts. "Thanks to Him, the God and Father of our Lord Jesus Christ ... the God from whom all help comes. He helps us in all our troubles, so that we are able to help others in all kinds of troubles, using the same help that we ourselves have received from God" (2 Cor. 1:3-4).

[2]   *God was a Stranger* by Margaret Kirk (OMF Books).

J.O. Sanders, *an OMF Consulting Director, and now in his eighties, is still being used by God in a wide-ranging Bible ministry throughout the world.*

The Right To Choose the Colours

She was a charming, vivacious seventeen-year-old. Life had been kind to her. She was intelligent, popular, artistic, athletic, and romance was waiting around the corner. Life's prospects were entrancing. Everything seemed to be going her way.

Suddenly, as the outcome of a sporting accident, she found herself paralyzed from the neck down — a paraplegic! If ever it could be said that the roof of a life had caved in, surely this was it. The tragedy was complete and irreversible. What could life hold for her but endless limitation and frustration? And yet, out of what appeared to be unrelieved tragedy, there has grown a world-encircling ministry of comfort and encouragement to a host of sufferers.

The subject of this traumatic experience was Joni Eareckson, now known around the world for her books, her art work and the spoken word. Thousands have reason to bless her for the way in which her triumph over tragedy has pointed the pathway for them to meet and overcome their own shattering experiences.

"When I first began realizing all the adjustments that being paralyzed involves," she wrote, "I thought to myself, 'My lot in life is harder than anyone else's. How many people have the humiliation of needing someone else to bathe them? What other girl can't even scratch her own shoulder and comb her own hair?'

"I desperately wanted to kill myself. Here I was, trapped in this canvas cocoon. I couldn't move anything except my head. Physically I was little more than a corpse. I had no hope of ever walking again. I could never lead a normal life and marry Dick."[1] How bleak the prospect!

Yet in retrospect Joni bore this testimony: "Today as I look back, I am convinced that the whole ordeal of my paralysis was inspired by God's love. God had *reasons* behind my suffering, and learning some of them has made all the difference in the world."

In most lives there comes, sooner or later, a devastating crisis, a time when the roof caves in. For long periods life flows along smoothly with only minor ripples on its surface. Joys and sorrows are fairly evenly balanced, and life is pleasant and fulfilling.

Then, without warning, out of the blue tragedy strikes and everything falls apart. The shattering

[1] *A Step Further*, Joni Eareckson, pp 13, 15.

crisis may take one of many forms — the sudden death of a dearly loved one; a terminal illness; sudden physical incapacity; a motor accident; a business collapse; a divorce or separation; unemployment; a moral failure; a broken engagement; birth of a handicapped child; a child on drugs. Our sun goes into eclipse, the future seems intolerable and the thought of what lies ahead almost beyond our capacity to bear it.

How are we to cope with such unwelcome intrusions into the even tenor of life? It must be said that there is no rule of thumb, no easy solution. We must face the facts realistically and look to God in confident, albeit tearful trust to see us through. Nor will He fail us.

It is helpful to recall that, although it may seem so to us, our experience is not unique. Hundreds of others have faced similar tragedy and emerged enriched rather than impoverished by the experience. What has been their secret?

A study of both biblical and contemporary life-stories reveals that the important factor is not so much the severity of the crisis and its devastating effects, as the manner in which we handle it.

A lady was talking with a recently-widowed friend. In the course of conversation she remarked, "Sorrow does colour life, doesn't it?" "Yes, it does indeed," rejoined the other, "*but I intend to choose the colours!*" The right to choose the colours is always within our power.

The Bible is the most realistic and contemporary of books. It preserves the biographies of repre-

sentative men and women and records real life
situations, but always with specific ends in view.
Bible biographies are not merely history, but
history with definite lessons for succeeding generations.

For example, in referring to that memorable trek
of the Hebrews from Egypt, through the desert and
into the Promised Land, Paul gives the reason for
the preservation of that piece of history: "Now these
things occurred as examples to keep us from setting
our hearts on evil things as they did .... These
things happened to them as examples, *and were
written down as warnings for us on whom the fulfilment of
the ages has come*" (1 Cor. 10:6, 11).

A Greek sage once said that the proper study of
mankind is man. And who better could we select for
our study than those whose biographies have been
preserved by divine inspiration? In keeping with
the sincerity of Bible biography, failures are as
frankly dealt with as successes, and the causes of
each faithfully disclosed.

Let us consider some biblical characters, and
learn what we can from the way in which they
reacted when the roof caved in. This will afford
helpful insights into the principles of successful
Christian living, and bring inspiration and encouragement to those battling amid the tests of
present-day life.

The mystery of undeserved suffering

Job was certainly one who gained his graduate's
degree in the school of suffering. Despite the pro-

testations of his professed friends, the multiplied trials and tragedies which overtook him were not the result of failure and sin on his part. He had to face and cope with the mystery of seemingly unmerited suffering. And while this great epic poem does not provide a final answer to that problem, it does throw considerable light on the special purpose suffering is intended to serve in the life of the upright. It demonstrates the glorious possibility of a Christian maintaining a full consecration to God, even when the roof is caving in on him.

In a few terse words Job is depicted as "blameless and upright. He feared God and shunned evil" (1:1). "He was the greatest man among all the people of the East" (1:3). His great wealth was regarded by his contemporaries as a sign that he enjoyed the signal favour of God. His domestic picture was one of happy and relaxed conviviality. He displayed a deep solicitude for the moral and spiritual welfare of his family (1:4,5). It would be difficult to imagine a happier lot than his. But he had yet to be tested by terrible and unexplained disaster.

Overnight, everything fell apart. In quick succession flocks and herds, servants and sons and daughters were swept away (1:13-19). But the hour of trauma and tragedy only served to reveal the true calibre of the man. Caught totally unawares, he reacted like one who knew his God:

"At this, Job got up and tore his robe and shaved his head. Then he fell to the ground in worship and said, 'Naked I came from my mother's womb, and naked I will depart. The Lord gave and the Lord has taken away; may the name of the Lord be praised'" (1:20-22).

His noble reaction to tragedy won the approval of God (2:3), but it also aroused the malignity of Satan. One of the important insights we gain from this drama is that events on earth may have an unsuspected background in the heavenly realm. For a brief moment the curtain is drawn aside and we are permitted a glimpse into the court of heaven. It was in this gathering that Job's mounting crescendo of trial had its origin.

Satan sneeringly suggested that God was naive to suppose Job's integrity and loyalty to Him were disinterested. He was loyal only because of the benefits he received. In any case, Satan alleged, God had put a hedge of privilege around Job (1:9-11). Thus he threw down the gauntlet. God accepted the challenge, removed the hedge and gave Satan permission to put Job to the test, but within strictly prescribed limits (1:12).

Calamity after calamity overwhelmed the patriarch. Though he was broken in heart and broken in body, "in all this, Job did not sin by charging God with wrongdoing" (1:22). Satan had lost the first round.

But he had other tricks in his bag. He struck Job with a disease so loathsome that he was banished from the city to the ash heap outside its walls (2:8). So unbearable was the suffering that he longed for nothing more than death. From being the greatest man of the East, he had become an outcast on the ash heap! From the purely human angle there seemed justification for his wife's bitter jibe: "Are you still holding on to your integrity? Curse God and die!" (2:9).

"You are talking like a foolish woman", rejoined Job. "Shall we accept good from God and not trouble?" The greatness of the man shone through in his noble reply. Once again it is recorded that "in all this, Job did not sin in what he said." Satan had lost his second round.

Francis Xavier might have had Job in mind when he penned these words:

My God, I love Thee, not because
I hope for heaven thereby,
Nor yet because who love Thee not
Are lost eternally;
Not from the hope of gaining aught,
Not seeking a reward;
But as Thyself hast loved me,
O ever-loving Lord.

The high point of the whole story is reached when Job, after the majestic vision of God had brought him to his knees, humbly made this confession: "I know that you can do all things, no plan of yours can be thwarted .... My ears had heard of you, but now my eyes have seen you. Therefore I despise myself and repent in dust and ashes" (42:1,5,6).

The saga closes with Job vindicated before Satan and his friends, and blessed with double what he had before. "The Lord blessed the latter part of Job's life more than the first" (42:12).

What an inspiring illustration of the way in which we can transform our trouble into treasure, and turn our sorrow into song!

When writing about the way the Christian should react when trouble shakes the very foundations of life, William Barclay had this to say:

"In that moment we turn to God because, as Lincoln said, there is nowhere else to go. But it will make all the difference in that moment, first, if we know where to go, and second, if through all the years we have kept our contact with God, and if we are going, not to a stranger but to a familiar Friend. In other words, the better we know God, the easier it is to go to Him when we need Him so desperately."[2]

The result of our own failure

Sometimes the crisis is the direct outcome of our own wrongdoing and sin. In such a case, if we are honest with ourselves, we will acknowledge that fact and accept the consequent trauma as the just reward of our deeds. God will not condone sin in a Christian any more than He does in an unbeliever. He allows results to take their own course. But how promptly He responds to the cry of His penitent child!

One cold night, as he warmed himself at the courtyard fire in Jerusalem's Judgement Hall, Peter's roof caved in.

Not long before, he had proudly boasted, "Even if I have to die with you, I will never disown you"

---

[2]   *Through the Bible with William Barclay*, p. 133.

(Matt. 26:35). But within a few days the story was very different:

"Now Peter was sitting out in the courtyard, and a servant girl came to him. 'You also were with Jesus of Galilee,' she said. But he denied it before them all ... After a little while, those standing there went up to Peter and said, 'Surely you are one of them, for your accent gives you away.'

"Then he began to call down curses on himself, and he swore to them, 'I don't know the man!'"

The shrill crowing of a rooster recalled to Peter the Lord's previous solemn warning. But it was when "the Lord turned and looked straight at Peter" — a look of wounded love, not of anger — that *"he went outside and wept bitterly."* It should be noted that it was the bitter tears rather than the shameful denial that were the true index of his heart attitude.

Once again his impetuous tongue had slipped the leash of his Master, and he who a few minutes before had attacked a raging mob single-handed to defend his Lord now capitulated before a girl's sneer. And now it was all over! The lovely dream had faded like the morning mist! He had shamefully failed his Lord in His hour of deepest need. All his hopes were dashed. He had forever forfeited his place in the apostolate. Back to the fishing business for him!

This is a standard reaction when the roof caves in on us as a result of our own sin and folly. But it was far from the end of the story. Peter had failed dismally, but he had yet to learn much of the pursuing love of the Master.

In Peter's restoration we are afforded comforting

insight into the Master's method with those who have failed and fallen. It was the look of forgiving love that began the process.

I saw One hanging on a tree,
In agonies and blood;
He fixed His languid eyes on me,
As near His cross I stood.
Sure, never to my dying breath
Can I forget that look;
It seemed to charge me with His death
Though not a word He spoke.

So wrote John Newton, the converted slave-trader, of his experience, and just so could Peter have written. That luminous look broke his heart and released a flood of salty tears. Not remorse or shame, not the memory of the futile warnings, but the look of ineffable love and compassion saved him from despair and worked a permanent repentance.

His repentance was real and deep, but no flood of tears could wash away his words of denial. He would have to live with them. Tears alone are not an adequate cathartic. He must pass through an experience so radical as to deliver him once and for all from the revealed weakness of his character.

This was achieved in the gracious interview specially arranged by the Lord after His resurrection. There he received his threefold commission from the Lord he had disowned (John 21:15-19). From that moment on he was securely and joyously chained to Christ's chariot wheel.

Who would have conceived that this same Peter would emerge from his abysmal fall as the leader of the one hundred and twenty in the upper room on the Day of Pentecost, and have primacy in the apostolate? Only Jesus could see in the cursing fisherman the chosen preacher of the most vital sermon ever delivered in the history of the Christian church. It was to Peter that the risen Lord entrusted the keys that would open the Kingdom of God to both Jew and Gentile.

So take courage, my brother, my sister who have experienced tragic failure. The arms of a forgiving God are open to you, and the door to future service is not slammed in your face.

The mystery of unexplained discipline

"When the Lord exalts His servants to positions of importance it is because He has prepared them by discipline." This was very true in the case of Joseph, who for thirteen years had to wrestle with the problem of continuing and unexplained tragedy. For him the roof caved in several times.

As a promising adolescent, he was spoiled by an aging and indulgent father. Much in his early life appears less than humble and noble. The even tenor of his life was rudely disturbed when he was sold to the Midianites and became one of a long line of fettered slaves (Gen. 37). But all unknown to him there was a kindly providence overruling the seeming tragedy. He had yet to learn that

All is of God that is, and is to be;

And God is good! (J.G. Whittier)

His sale to the chief of Egypt's royal bodyguard was just the next hidden step on the road to undreamed of exaltation. His ability and high moral character soon won him advancement but he was still only a slave over slaves, even when he was made overseer of Potiphar's house and all that he had. Things were as favourable as they could be under the circumstances.

Then, suddenly, he found himself facing the most subtle and volcanic temptation of his life, in circumstances which were exquisitely difficult for virtue and tragically easy for moral laxity. It seemed as though everything had conspired to make sin easy and resistance next to impossible when the amoral wife of Potiphar made her suggestion. He was granted no time to brace himself for the shock.

The temptation gathered strength from the fact that it was totally unexpected, and came from an equally unexpected quarter. Resistance became more difficult because of the daily repetition of the temptation, and could easily have been worn down by persistence.

The secret of Joseph's victory lay largely in the fact that from the moment of the first shock he steadfastly refused to entertain any suggestion that would induce him to sin against God (Gen. 39:9). Many of his contemporaries would have laughed at his scruples, as ours do today; but to Joseph this was no mere peccadillo but "this great wickedness." He resolutely shut his eyes to worldly advantage and clung to moral principle — "How can I sin against God?" He had to pay a heavy price for his purity, but God gave abundant recompense in due time.

An analysis of his victory has important lessons for those who are in similar conditions of unexplained testing. The first is that his loyalty to his master was exceeded by his *loyalty and love for God*. To him, the essence of sin was that it was against God.

Then Joseph retained the *capacity of being shocked* by sin. Others regarded sin of that nature as just "having a little fling." "Our greatest security against sin is to be shocked by it," said E.M. Blaiklock.

Further, he was preserved in the sudden onslaught of temptation by his *habitual preparedness*. When it struck, he was walking in unbroken fellowship with God. In New Testament language, he was walking in the Spirit and so did not fulfil the desires of the flesh.

Lastly, his mind was *not conditioned for a fall*, as was that of David when he faced a similar test.

The superficial thinker and observer of life might conclude that Joseph's magnificient moral victory would be rewarded by some signal mark of God's favour and approval. Instead it was followed by yet further calamity. His faithfulness to God and His laws landed him in a dark dungeon. He might well have asked, "Does virtue pay? Does God care?" But though his faith was sorely tested as the months went by on leaden feet, it did not fail.

His imprisonment proved to be the divinely prepared stage for an incredible reward for faithfulness. He had taken his adversities in a submissive spirit, and instead of embittering they sweetened and ennobled him.

Then came the moment for which thirteen years

of mounting adversity had been unconsciously preparing him. His God-given wisdom in interpreting the Pharoah's dream and advising him how to act in the light of it, produced an immediate reaction in the heathen ruler:

"Since God has made all this known to you, there is no one so wise and discerning as you. You shall be in charge of my palace, and all my people are to submit to your orders. Only with respect to the throne will I be greater than you" (Gen. 41:38–40).

The disciplines of the hidden years had not been wasted. Now at length he could see unfolding before his astonished eyes the hidden plan of God. The mysterious links in the chain of providence became clearer. His imprisonment had been the essential step to his temporal advancement. His bitter experiences had been necessary to strengthen his nature so that he could hold his own with the stoutest men of Egypt.

> Behind our life the Weaver stands
>   And works His wondrous will;
> We leave it all in His wise hands
>   And trust His perfect skill.
> Should mystery enshroud His plan
>   And our short sight be dim,
> We will not try the whole to scan,
>   But leave each thread to Him.
>
> (C. Murray)

When Joseph made himself known to his brothers, he was able to make this remarkable confession of faith: "God sent me ahead of you to preserve for you a remnant on earth and to save your lives ..." (Gen.

45:7). "You intended to harm me, but God intended it for good ..." (Gen. 50:20).

An irreparably shattered career

But let us come back to the twentieth century in which all around us there are people, both Christian and non-Christian, who are in desperate trouble and do not know where to turn for help and guidance. I close this chapter with recounting the experience of one who suddenly found himself engulfed in one of the greatest political scandals of this century.

Few men of our generation have experienced such a traumatic cave-in as the men who were embroiled in the Watergate scandal which shook the whole political world. One of the chief among these was Charles (Chuck) Colson, who was often referred to as President Nixon's "hatchet man." He was an able, hard-hitting and apparently ruthless political executive in the White House. As such, he was among the most powerful men in the world.

"We were riding on the crest of the wave," he wrote. "Think of the power at our fingertips; a mere command from one of us could mobilize generals and cabinet officers, even armies; we could hire or fire personnel, and manage billions in agency budgets. Think of the privileges: a call to the military aide's office would produce a limousine or a jet aeroplane; red-jacketed stewards stood waiting to serve food and drink twenty-four hours a day; secret service men were always in sight, as many as we wanted."[3]

---

[3] *Loving God*, Charles Colson, p. 67.

He had reached the pinnacle of temporal power — and then the roof caved in. The powerful, self-confident Colson found himself with other convicts in prison, adjudged a criminal! How the mighty were fallen! He discovered that the valley was quite as deep as the mountain had been high.

It takes no vivid imagination to envisage the tremendous revulsion of feeling that his fall involved, not least of which were the repercussions on wife and family. From being one of the most powerful men in the nation, suddenly he was only a common convict. What could the future hold but shame and obloquy? How could one cope with a situation as tragic as that?

As the Watergate scandal exploded over the pages of the nation's press, Colson visited a long-time friend who surprised him by explaining that he had "accepted Jesus Christ." This rather shocked and baffled him, but it made him curious. His friend explained it all to him.

"That night I was confronted with my own sin — not just Watergate's dirty tricks, but the sin deep within me, the hidden evil, that lives in every heart. It was painful, I could not escape. I cried out to God, and found myself driven irresistibly into His waiting arms. That was the night I gave myself to Jesus Christ and began the greatest adventure of my life. A lot of skeptics thought it wouldn't last, that it was just a ploy for sympathy, a foxhole conversion ... But not once in these last ten years would I have turned the clock back. My lowest days as a Christian (and there were low ones — seven months' worth of them in prison to be exact) have been more fulfilling and rewarding than all the days of glory in the White House."[4]

When addressing his people in Jerusalem, Nehemiah asserted, "Our God turned the curse into a blessing" (Nehemiah 13:2). This is exactly what He did for Chuck Colson.

His bruising experience in prison developed in him a deep empathy with fellow-prisoners confined in penal institutions. On being released and once again able to enjoy the blessings of liberty, he did not selfishly hug that unspeakable boon. Instead he turned his thoughts to the tens of thousands of convicts and ex-convicts who had no one to minister to their spiritual destitution, and did not know the comfort of the salvation in which he now revelled.

He gathered around him a group of godly men with whom he shared his vision, and the outcome was the formation of *The Prison Fellowship*, an evangelical Christian organization geared to meet the spiritual needs of the convicts — and as far as possible, their temporal needs as well. Today he is known worldwide as the champion of the prisoner.

The movement has spread around the world, and thousands of criminals who had lost all hope of a better life have found hope, not alone in this life but also in the life to come. Christian men and women in many countries have been awakened to their social as well as their spiritual responsibilities, and are devoting themselves to leading prisoners to

[4]   *Loving God*, Charles Colson, p. 247.

Christ and helping to rehabilitate them in their new life.

When the roof caved in on Chuck Colson he was anything but a Christian, and to his dismay he discovered that he had no one to turn to for help in this hour of desperate need. But because an alert Christian friend, himself a new convert, was available to God in the hour of crisis, he was directed to the Saviour who forgave, cleansed and commissioned him. Unnumbered thousands are grateful to God that he has "not been disobedient to the heavenly vision." From the ruins of a shattered career, there has been born a ministry of compassion that circles the globe.

Other Helpful Books From OMF

WHEN GOD GUIDES — Living Testimonies Series
Does God guide individuals? Is guidance confined to the big things of life, or must I refer everything to His direction? In this book guidance is clothed in flesh and blood.

THE CLOUD AND THE SILVER LINING
— Denis Lane
International turmoil, refugees, corruption, fear and violence in the streets, a self-satisfied church deluding itself with humanistic theories, this was Judah in Ezekiel's day. Today too we need to hear Ezekiel's message.

IN HIS TIME compiled by Eileen L. Gordon-Smith
Ian Gordon-Smith lost his life in a mini-bus accident in Thailand along with eleven other missionaries and children. Although assured of a brilliant future at home he had been willing to sacrifice it in order to be obedient to the Lord he loved.

WALLS ARE FOR LEAPING — Dorothy Pape
An unforgettable account of the life of Michiko Tamura, who contracted polio as a small child on a far northern island of Japan taken over by Russia. She refused to be treated like an invalid and overcame prejudice against her deformity. After finding Christ she leaped over many impossible walls to help other handicapped Japanese, and even had a happy marriage.

SOMETIMES I PREFER TO FUSS — Verda Peet
Finally we have a book that captures the essence of ordinary missionary life. Sometimes painfully honest, often very funny and always realistic, Verda Peet offers a unique glimpse into cross-cultural missionary living.